Development through Technology Transfer

Creating new organisational and cultural understanding

Mohammed Saad

intellect™
Bristol, UK
Portland, OR, USA

First Published in Great Britain in Hardback in 2000 by
Intellect Books, PO Box 862, Bristol BS99 1DE, UK

First Published in USA in 2000 by
Intellect Books, ISBS, 5824 N.E. Hassalo St, Portland, Oregon 97213-3644, USA

Consulting Editor: Masoud Yazdani
Copy Editor: Ann Marangos
Production: Sally Ashworth & Robin Beecroft
Cover Illustration: Julie Payne

A catalogue record for this book is available from the British Library

ISBN 1-84150-028-3

Printed and bound in Great Britain by Cromwell Press, Wiltshire

Contents

Foreword

'Technology makes the world go round'. Somewhat simplistic but this statement (from a manager of a large company) and countless others from politicians, academics, consultants and businesses underlines two key themes which will dominate the 21st century. Technological change – as has so often been the case – will act as the motor for much economic development and play a key part in shaping the ways in which the world develops. But the revolutions which it will bring are increasingly unlikely to be confined to a particular region; in the future this will take place on a global stage. And the consequence of this is that actors in the economic system – policy-makers, researchers, practitioners – will need to develop skills in understanding and managing the process of technological change.

In this book, Mohammed Saad investigates the process of technology transfer into developing countries. His particular contribution to knowledge in this important field is twofold. First, he is one of few researchers to locate technology transfer within the theories and frameworks of innovation management. Secondly, his approach is practically focused on individual firms and the ways in which they acquire new knowledge and learn how to learn.

Dr Saad demonstrates how to avoid costly mistakes and how to make the most of critical investments in advanced technology. The central theme is the interaction between organisational learning and technological adaptation. The book is an important and timely contribution to the emerging fields of technology transfer and sustainable development. Given the above concerns it should be required reading for academics, managers and policy-makers in both developing and industrialised countries.

John Bessant
Professor of Technology Management and Director of the Centre for Research in Innovation Management (CENTRIM) at Brighton Business School, University of Brighton.

Acknowledgements

I owe the completion of *Development through Technology Transfer* to many people upon whom I relied for help and encouragement while it was being written. My heartfelt thanks go to my family in Algeria and especially to my wife Saliha and my two wonderful daughters Nadia and Hassina for being so supportive and understanding throughout the whole time it took to complete writing this book. I must also thank my colleagues from the School of Operations Management of Bristol Business School for their advice, ideas and patience, with special thanks to Beulah Cope, Margaret Greenwood, Ian Holden and Peter James. Thanks also go to my friends and colleagues Gareth Lewis, Annie Lewis and George Mann for their comments and critiques.

I would like to express my gratitude to workers and managers of NEEI and NEFM and other friends from Algeria for the countless meetings and discussions we had together. I also owe a debt of gratitude to friends and ex-colleagues from the Centre for Innovation in Management at Brighton University, whose help at the initial stage of the research was extremely valuable. Among them I especially want to mention John Bessant, Howe Rush and Karamjit Gill.

This book is dedicated to the memory of my mother and my brother Ali who died too soon to know of its existence.

Mohammed Saad
Bristol Business School, University of the West of England

Introduction

Technological change is a key factor in economic growth, industrial change and international competitiveness. It is the major component responsible for increases in output and income in most industrialised countries.

In most developing countries, the basic source of industrial development, knowledge and technological change comes from industrialised countries through a process known as technology transfer. This process, which constitutes the principal means of incorporating technical change within the productive infrastructure of developing countries is defined as the application of new technology to a new use or user for economic gain (Rodrigues, 1985). It refers to a wide area of activities such as product, process, cost reduction, integration of local materials and import substitution, employee involvement, improvement of safety and working conditions. It can be product-embodied, process-embodied or personnel-embodied (Chen, 1996). Consequently, technology transfer is, like innovation, a new idea which is not trivial to an organisation.

In the specific context of developing countries, Cooper (1980) claims that innovation is the introduction of a process or a product that is new to the economy of that particular country, regardless of whether it has been used before elsewhere. It includes all modifications or adaptations of processes or products that are new, however minor they may be. Innovation in developing countries is also often associated with the implementation, adaptation and management of technology and is mainly concerned with:

i.   new product innovation;
ii.   process innovation;
iii.   minor modifications whose objectives are cost reduction, plant capacity utilisation, production time reduction, quality improvement, etc;
iv.   integration of local components (import-substitution);
v.   improvement of safety and working conditions;
vi.   employee involvement;
vii.   organisation and management;
viii.   major changes involving investments in additional and/or new product facilities.

Similar to the concept of innovation, technology transfer is any idea which can lead to enhanced performance and is related to various activities, actors and variables.

To survive in a context characterised by high competition and constant change, organisations from both developed and developing countries have no other alternative except to innovate. However, technology transfer, like innovation, is a risky and complex activity. Both convey a great deal of uncertainty made up of technical, market, social, political and cultural factors and success is not always guaranteed.

In addition, and although a great deal has already been learned about the innovation process through which technological change is leading to economic growth and development, most of these studies have been undertaken in the context of developed countries.

This book represents an attempt to gain further understanding of the process of technology transfer by making reference to the innovation process. This can help identify those elements of technology transfer in developing countries which fit the theoretical framework of innovation and provide an analytical model to examine the key stages of the process of technology transfer, its diffusion and key determinants, and shape the way in which it needs to be managed.

As technology transfer involves the whole process whereby knowledge related to the transfer of inputs into outputs is acquired, its effective management is increasingly associated with continuously acquiring and mobilising knowledge and technological skills (Chen, 1996; Tidd *et al.*, 1997). Success, as shown in the following figure, depends on generating new knowledge and on having the capabilities to react quickly and effectively to change. This book supports this view. It considers the process of transfer of technology as being more than the hand-over of new technological hardware and focuses on relatively under-examined issues related to learning and managing technology.

The purpose of this book is to examine the process of the transfer of technology in developing countries, through case studies drawn from the Algerian experience. It aims to highlight the key stages of this process and to identify the facilitating and

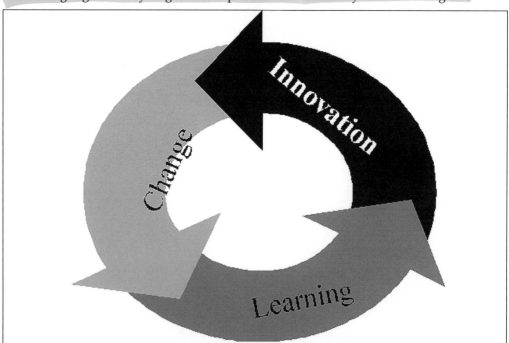

Managing change through innovation and learning

constraining factors to the acquisition of technology and to the development of indigenous technological capabilities.

The Algerian experience represents an example of a developing country striving to establish an important industrial base as rapidly as possible through a programme of massive investment. Its strategy for technology transfer has been based essentially on the combination of hardware and software models with the use of turnkey and product-in-hand contracts in the 1970s, followed by 'decomposed' contracts in the 1980s. This study focuses mainly on the period 1966 to 1990 and aims to examine the pattern adopted by firms from developing countries in the management of the process of technology transfer and the development of their technological capabilities.

Chapter 1 explores and analyses the ways in which innovation has been approached and defined and scrutinises the continuous debate over the causes of innovation. It aims to outline the determinants for a successful implementation of innovation and to explore the relevance of the theories of innovation in the context of developing countries. Chapter 2 reviews the literature on technology transfer in developing countries. It highlights the critical elements which affect the implementation and the management of this process from the recipient perspective. Chapter 3 examines the effectiveness of the main strategies for technology transfer adopted by developing countries such as Algeria in their attempt to establish a strong industrial basis and develop their economy. Chapters 4 and 5 bring the discussion to the level of firms and examine the acquisition and use of conventional and new technology in two state-owned enterprises. The objective is to identify and analyse the pattern adopted by both companies in the development of their technological capabilities. It also identifies the facilitating and constraining factors for implementing innovation in developing countries. Chapter 6 reviews the degree of appropriateness of organisational arrangements used by such companies in successfully acquiring and implementing new technology. Chapter 7, which defines technology transfer as a dynamic process of learning, focuses on the learning processes of the case-study examples in order to evaluate their pattern of technological development and determine if this pattern has followed any of the models defined by the literature review.

Chapter 8 focuses on the effective acquisition and operation of advanced technology by challenging the traditional, Fordist model of organisation used in developing countries. It aims to explore the possibility to enhance performance through new forms of organisation that can be simple to adopt and assimilate.

Chapter 9 highlights the complex and dynamic nature of the technology transfer which requires for its successful implementation effective and continuous learning and organisational adaptations.

Chapter 1
Innovation Process and Influential Factors

This chapter explores and analyses the ways innovation has been approached and defined. A first section is devoted to the historical evolution of technology. The objective of this section is to examine the major attempts used to explain technological changes as an evolutionary process. The second section explores the nature of innovative activity and highlights its complexity and its multi-disciplinary approach. The third section focuses on the intricate aspect of this activity by examining the whole innovation process. The fourth section scrutinises the continuous debate over the causes of innovation and finally the fifth section outlines the determinants for a successful implementation of innovation. In conclusion, this chapter examines the relevance of these theories in the context of developing countries.

1. Historical Evolution of Technological Changes

Classical economists, from Adam Smith to Milton Friedman, have presented the history of technology as a continuous process of advance. In general, economists have always recognised the importance of technological change in the promotion of economic growth. For Adam Smith in 1776, the division of labour and improvements in machinery led to the promotion of invention. Marx in 1848 stated the necessity for the bourgeoisie to revolutionise constantly the means of production. It was, however, Schumpeter and Schmookler who identified technological change as an important component of economic development.

In a paper published in 1952, Schmookler stated the belief that the growth in the national product of the USA in the 70-year period leading up to 1938 was due not only to the growth in the stock of capital and labour but also to the growth of efficiency in the use of these resources. Kuznets (1965) supported this view, which found its greatest advocates in Solow (1957) and Kendrick (1984). According to them, from about 1900 to 1920 'technical progress' as Solow called it or 'productivity advance' as Kendrick termed it, contributed 1% a year to the rise in the national output of the USA, and between 1920 and 1950 this contribution increased to 2% per year. Solow added that no more than 1/8 of the growth of output per head could be attributed to increased capital input, and the remaining 7/8 should be credited to technical progress. Thus, the major breakthrough was that the growth in output was the result of factors believed to be entirely due to technological progress.

The history of technology appears as one of steady progress from the time of the Industrial Revolution. The primary Industrial Revolution, concerned with the development of steam energy, was followed by a series of secondary revolutions (railway, electricity and electronics). One of the first and major contributions to this theory of long-term economic development and structural change in capitalist societies came from Joseph Schumpeter.

1.1. Schumpeter's Contribution

Schumpeter' s theory of economic development contained an important evolutionary trait which according to Coombs *et al*.(1987) represented a radical departure from neoclassical economics. The primary concern of the neoclassical school was to explain and predict changes in the relationships between static economic variables such as prices, output and profit in the general equilibrium model based on the assumption of maximisation and perfect competition. For Schumpeter, innovation was the main driving force of change giving rise to the growth and decline of economies. In his concern about the ways economic systems respond to perturbations, Schumpeter adopted an evolutionary model in which technological change and the efficacy of the entrepreneur as an innovative agent played the most significant role.

Indeed, in his study of capitalism, in which innovation is defined as 'the main engine of capitalist growth and the source of entrepreneurial profit' Schumpeter suggested that 'the essential point to grasp is that in dealing with capitalism we are dealing with an evolutionary process'. He also added that 'capitalism can never be stationary'. Thus, Schumpeter was a strong defender of the theory that the supply of innovation is more important than the adaptation to existing patterns of demand. Schumpeter viewed the entrepreneur as being the key character in capitalist societies, often discovering new ideas and introducing them into economic life. However, after having identified in his early work in 1912 the individual entrepreneur as the source of innovation, Schumpeter argued in his later works in 1928 and 1939 that it is the entrepreneurial function which generated innovation rather that the individual entrepreneur.

In his study of business cycles (1934, 1939, 1942), Schumpeter came to recognise that 'every concrete process of development finally rests upon preceding development' and 'every process of development creates the pre-requisites for the following'. These notions of cumulative and pre-requisite development show Schumpeter's acknowledgement of cycles in economic development. In this context, Schumpeter took up Kondratiev's work and introduced the idea of technological revolution as the basis of the 'Kondratiev cycles'.

In the 1920s, Kondratiev of the Institute of Applied Economic Research in Moscow was among the first to attempt to collect data to clarify the turning point of the long cycles. Kondratiev saw these cycles being related to the durability of certain types of investment such as buildings and transport. In his study of business cycles, Schumpeter added that innovations causing economic fluctuations are evenly distributed through time and appear discontinuously in groups or 'swarms'. From Kondratiev's work, Schumpeter identified the following waves.

i.   The first 'Kondratiev wave' from 1785 to 1845 and which corresponds to steampower.
ii. The railways as the second 'Kondratiev wave' from 1845 to 1900.
iii. The third 'Kondratiev wave' from 1900 to 1950 corresponding to electric power and the automobile.

In spite of the significant evolutionary feature carried in his theory of economics, Schumpeter was also influenced by the Walrasian theory of 'equilibrium'. This explains why Schumpeter started his analysis from a state of equilibrium which gets thrown into disequilibrium. He therefore held the view that innovation generates disequilibrium. Indeed, Schumpeter classified economic cycles in the following ways: prosperity, recession, depression and revival.

In the prosperity period innovation is successful and risk is cut down. As a consequence a shift from equilibrium occurs. In the recession, the innovative impetus ends and the stage returns to a new equilibrium. The depression appears when former innovation has no effect. Finally, the revival emerges when new innovations are introduced into the market.

However, in his study of business cycles, Schumpeter emphasised further his evolutionary approach and defined economic evolution as being about 'changes in the process brought about by innovation, together with all their effects and the responses to them by the economic system'. As Juma (1986) points out, this view of evolutionary theory 'transcends the notion of circular economic flows and the tendency towards general equilibrium'. Indeed the disequilibrium caused by innovation opens up new opportunities for adaptation which leads to new innovation. Schumpeter viewed this as 'the setting up of a new production function'. For Freeman (1974), Schumpeter held the view that innovations generate disequilibrium first because innovations are unevenly distributed since they tend to concentrate in certain specific sectors and second innovations 'cluster' come about in 'bunches' as a result of the diffusion process which is also uneven. While Schumpeter's contribution to the understanding of the role of innovation in the process of economic change is widely acknowledged, it is, however, argued that he ignored the process of innovation itself. Usher (1954) and Strassman (1959) point out that Schumpeter's work was merely a description of the consequences of innovation and did not explain the process. For Ruttan (1959) and Freeman (1996) there was nothing in Schumpeter's work that could be identified as a theory of innovation. He had very little to say about the origin of innovations or about the management of innovation at the micro-level. Kuznets (1965) and Perez (1984) asserted that Schumpeter provided no explanation of the mechanisms of causation which underlay the activity of innovation. Kuznets argued that both Schumpeter and Kondratiev had failed to substantiate their theories by reference to statistics on production, trade and employment.

In line with Schumpeter, the neo-Schumpeterian school has explained the role of innovation in the process of economic development, but has also attempted to explain the process of innovation itself.

1.2. Major Neo-Schumpeterian Contributions

In this section, the neo-Schumpeterian work is divided into three groups. The first includes works from Mensch (1979), Freeman (1974) and Freeman and Perez (1988) where emphasis is placed upon long economic cycles. The second group comprises the work of Nelson and Winter (1977,1978,1982) which deals with search and selection mechanisms. The last group is devoted to the 'Organic' approach to innovation proposed by Clark and Juma (1987), Rothwell (1992), Kanter (1996), Morgan (1997) and Tidd *et al.* (1997).

For all three groups, technology is the major factor generating economic change, and technological change is an evolutionary process which is interactive, cumulative, institutional and disequilibrating.

Long Cycles Theory

Mensch (1979) proposed a theory of 'bunching' of basic innovation to explain how Kondratiev waves start. He claims that historically such a pattern can be observed to occur in the depression periods of the 1830s, 1880s, 1930s and he predicted a new cluster of basic innovation in the 1980s. The cycles according to Mensch (1979) are associated with a cluster of basic innovations which establish new branches of industry. The resulting economic expansion reaches a limit and consequently a technological stalemate is reached. Mensch argues that the stalemate creates an 'accelerator mechanism' and hence induces innovations which come again in clusters and boost the economy. Thus, during the technological stalemate of the recession phase, the basic or radical innovations are crowded out, providing the opportunity for subsequent recovery.

This theory was challenged by Freeman and his colleagues (1982). They argue that 'once swarming does start it has powerful multiplier effects in generating additional demand in the economy for capital goods, for materials, components, distribution facilities and of course labour'. This induces a further wave of process and applications innovations, and gives rise to expansionary effects in the economy as a whole. It is, according to Freeman *et al.* (1982) the effect of swarming that leads to economic expansion, and not depression inducement as suggested by Mensch. However, Freeman and his colleagues acknowledge that depression may bring about institutional, political and social changes which can facilitate the adoption of new systems of technology.

Freeman and Perez (1988) introduced the notion of a 'techno-economic paradigm' which is much wider than clusters of innovations or even of technology systems. These two authors use the concept of a paradigm as Kuhn (1962) does to describe a way of seeing a dominant pattern which influences thinking across a very broad front. Kuhn introduced new ways of looking at the development of knowledge in general, and scientific knowledge in particular. He argued that scientific knowledge did not develop in a linear progression but in a series of historical stages of stability and disruption leading to periodic paradigm shifts in which the whole structure of how scientists see the world is altered. However, Kuhn did not examine the socio-economic context which shapes the emergence of particular paradigms.

This concept of a techno-economic paradigm, as defined by Freeman and Perez (1988), refers to 'a combination of interrelated products embodying a quantum jump in potential productivity for all or most of the economy and opening up an usually wide range of investment and profit opportunities'. This quantum jump in productivity is seen by Perez (1984) as 'a technological revolution, which is made possible by the appearance in the general cost structure of a particular input or key factor'. Thus, each mode of development would be influenced by a specific technological style or paradigm for the most efficient organisation of production (Freeman, 1996). By technological style we mean an ideal type of productive organisation or a best practice pattern which develops as a response to what are perceived as the stable dynamics of the relative cost structure for a given period of capitalist development. This assumes a strong feedback interaction between the economic, social and institutional spheres which generate a dynamic complementarity centred around a technological style. Thus the structural crisis which affects the economic as well as the socio-institutional spheres requires the adaptation of the socio-institutional context to innovations leading to a new technological style. This is why Freeman and Perez (1988) suggest that the favourable conditions for their paradigm should include 'complementarities between innovations and the emergence of an appropriate infrastructure as well as some degree of political stability and institutions which do not hinder too much the diffusion of new technologies'.

Such a paradigm has a major influence on the behaviour of the entire economy. For Freeman and Perez, 'it not only leads to the emergence of a new range of products, services, systems and industries ... it also affects directly or indirectly almost every other branch of the economy'.

The techno-economic paradigm consists of a combination of radical and incremental, innovations and its emergence is basically justified by the scope of changes brought about by technology. Radical innovations are the result of deliberate Research and Development (R&D) activity and are discontinuous events. Conversely, incremental innovations occur more or less continuously depending upon a combination of demand pressures, socio-cultural factors, technological opportunities and trajectories. The incremental innovations occur essentially as the outcome of simple improvements suggested by users as the result of their 'learning-by-doing'. These incremental innovations which do not require a high level of in-house skill, are viewed by Bell (1982, 1984) and others as being the most appropriate to firms from developing countries.

Freeman and Perez's (1988) techno-economic paradigm is also based on organisational and managerial innovations since the changes involved affect not only engineering activities but also various facets of management activities such as production, distribution and organisation. Thus each wave is not only concerned with technological clusters but has also dominant organisational forms associated with it. This explains Bessant's (1990) suggestion of a fifth wave in which emphasis is put on the following features.

i.   non-price factors;
ii.   flexibility in technology;
iii.   flexibility in organisational structure;
iv.   changing relationships within and between organisations;

This techno-economic paradigm acknowledges the necessity to surmount the incompatibility between the emergence of new technology and the older forms of organisation based on division of labour and rigid bureaucratic style which characterise the fourth wave known as mass-production or the Fordist-Paradigm.

Freeman and Perez explained technological changes as an evolutionary process in which emphasis was put on long economic cycles. Their study was, however, limited to the macro-level and was hardly brought to the level of the organisation nor to the context of developing countries.

Search and Selection Theories

The works of Nelson and Winter (1977, 1978, 1982), which contributed to a better understanding of innovation at the organisational level, are acknowledged as being of notable value in the search and selection approach. They define innovation as 'a change of decision rules' and argue that such 'a change in decision rules is more likely to be stimulated by threats and adversities than by a situation characterised by favourable outcomes'. Thus according to Nelson and Winter, organisations that are sufficiently profitable do not search for alternative techniques. The search for innovation may only happen when there is a pressure of threats, such as adversity. These 'decision rules' are known as technological trajectories, that organisations embrace them and may change them depending on the characteristics of their products and processes, and on the environment in which the organisation operates.

The notion of search and selection, which is central to Nelson and Winter's work, assumes the pre-existence of technological possibilities. Their model rests on the following three concepts.

i.   Organisations have a set of organisational routines which set out what is to be done and how it is done. This routine is considered to be the genetic code of the firm, it stores information and is used for search processes. They carry the adaptive information required for competition and survival. Thus, the information in the genetic code changes over time with experiences.

ii.   Organisations undertake a search process for possible modifications or replacements which generates innovation.

iii.   The third concept is the selection environment, this includes all the factors which influence the well-being of the organisation and covers both the conditions prevailing outside the organisation including the behaviour of other organisations.

Nelson and Winter contend that the choice of innovation is basically purposive but they consider the generation of innovation as rather stochastic. However, Nelson and Winter's paradigm is defined not only in terms of opportunity and the appropriateness of the conditions but also in terms of cumulativeness of innovation and in terms of nature and learning procedures. For Pavitt (1984a, 1984b, 1985 and 1987), Nelson and Winter (1982) and Rosenberg (1976, 1979, 1982), organisations are more likely to search into areas which are proximate to their accumulated experience and capabilities. Lundvall (1990) and Nelson (1993) describe this selection environment as a 'national system of innovation'. This describes the complex nature of institutions and policies which influence and shape the process of innovation and technology at micro-level in any particular national economy.

Thus, the technological approach adopted by a firm will not be static but rather flexible to new requirements and will not be similar to those adopted by other firms operating in the same industry. Nelson and Winter's work places emphasis upon mechanisms arising at the level of the organisation. Such a theory may therefore imply the possibility of defining an approach specific to organisations from industrialising countries where the innovation process, the determinants of this process, the organisational competencies and the 'national system of innovation' can differ from those characterising the developed countries. Each situation can generate its own approach taking into account interactions between technology, science, society, market and local requirements. However, the search for new solutions to particular problems as suggested by Nelson and Winter involves various learning procedures as well as search processes based on R&D activities (Rothwell et *al.*, 1976; Cooper, 1980; Pavitt, 1987). As mentioned earlier, firms from developing countries, with a low level of in-house skills, are often unable to undertake R&D activities and would instead tend to search for new solutions by merely using learning approaches[1] like 'learning-by-doing' and 'learning-by-using', which lead to incremental and continuous accumulation of experience in production and use.

Nelson and Winter's theory aims to avoid generalisations from one industry to another or from one firm to another since that each firm is normally committed to a specific technology and operates in a specific context.

The Organic Approach

Another approach known as the organic approach was proposed by Clark and Juma (1987) in which the concept of interaction between science, technology, society, market and local requirements is amplified. This approach is based on the General System Theory that unifies static structures and dynamic evolution in one general framework. Clark and Juma see innovation as an evolutionary process which is cumulative through time within the social system. They argue that organisations conducting or facilitating innovation require time to gain capability, experience, knowledge and information in order to formulate change and adjust their conduct and policy. Indeed Clark and Juma assert that it is not only organisations which generate innovative activities but also the 'network' between firms, subcontractors and government institutions. They illustrate their view by an example from the study of photovoltaic technology which shows that 'institutions are major facilitators of technical evolution'. They further explain that 'not only do the institutions provide financial support for the generation of technical variations but they also shape the selection mechanism'. The institutions provide the feedback mechanisms between external environments and technical development necessary for the generation of innovation. Clark and Juma place emphasis on innovation to be seen as a process instead of a fixed entity moving through economic space. The significance and influence of interactions and feedback mechanisms on the development of innovation are further explored by the new and recent literature on innovation in which the debate has shifted from an emphasis on internal structure to external linkages and processes (Tidd *et al.*, 1997).

Greater importance is increasingly being placed upon the importance of inter-organisation linkages and the structures of the public and private sector context within which innovation prospers (Rothwell, 1992; Cooke and Morgan, 1993; Marceau, 1996).

This research focus is explained by the successful emergence of innovation in industries such as consumer electronics, which was mainly based on inter-firm collaboration and the development of networks, sometimes sponsored by governments. Networks are increasingly being used to respond rapidly to fast-changing needs through the pooling of resources and the sharing of risk (Hobbay, 1996). This form of collaboration can assist in dealing with growing environmental uncertainty and complexity resulting from globalisation of markets and rapidly changing technologies (Granstrand *et al.*, 1992). It is also seen as a means to facilitate learning, transfer of technology and innovation (Dodgson, 1996).

The significance of the spatial or geographical dimension of innovation is motivated by the need to understand and acknowledge the successful development of innovative capacity associated with specific locations such as Silicon Valley in California and Emilia-Romagna in Northern Italy. This research has highlighted the importance of concepts such as 'industrial districts, 'innovative milieux' and 'regional innovation networks' (Porter, 1990; Camgni, 1991; Cooke and Morgan, 1993; Kanter, 1995). The emergence of regional concentrations of innovation has reinforced the view that innovation is a collective process which depends on many different interactions between an organisation and its external environment,which includes suppliers, customers, technical institutes, training bodies, technology transfer agencies, trade associations and other government agencies, etc.

In line with the neo-Schumpeterian research, the new literature also supports the idea of adopting a multidisciplinary and integrated approach in trying to evaluate effectively the innovative potential of an organisation, an industry, a region or a nation. The value for such an integrated approach is that it implies that innovation should be seen not as a separate activity, but as a whole, integrating the organisation with its entire external environment (Grindley, 1993).

The neo-Schumpeterian research places great emphasis on aspects which include the cumulative aspects of technology, the importance of incremental as well as radical innovations and the multiple inputs to innovation from diverse sources within and outside the firm. For the neo-Schumpeterians, innovation is an evolutionary process which is cumulative, interactive, institutional and disequilibrating. It is a highly complex phenomenon where changes are of techno-economic and social types since they affect not only engineering activities but also institutions and various facets of management and organisation activities.

Many studies, both theoretical and empirical, have been carried out in order to identify the causes and the factors likely to generate innovation. But, although this research has significantly improved the understanding of the intricate relationships which cause technological change, there is still not a satisfactory explanation of the origin of innovations. The sources and the process of innovation are rarely confined within the boundaries of individual organisations. This explains the complex and uncertain aspect of innovation, which requires the combination of inputs from a multiplicity of sources.

2. Models of Innovation

This section aims to investigate the nature of the innovative activity by reviewing the major elements of the debate about the causes of innovation. Early theories described innovation as a linear process comprising a succession of functional activities. Subsequent models viewed innovation as a coupling and matching activity marked by a multi-factor process which requires high levels of interaction and integration at intra- and inter-organisation levels.

2.1. Linear Model: Technology-Push versus Need-Pull Model

The dominant model of innovation has been for a long time the linear model, according to which innovation is a sequence of stages starting either from scientific research (Technology-Push) or some perception of a demand (Need-Pull model). It was the work of Schumpeter and Schmookler that first placed the emphasis on technology as a primary engine of growth. Coombs *et al*. (1987) consider the work of these two economists as central to contemporary theories. For both of them, although in quite different ways, technological change was a very important component of economic development.

The work of Schumpeter initiated the major hypothesis of the Technology-Push model – that it is only by introducing radically new ideas into economic life that development can be generated. This model of innovation emphasised scientific and technological advance, and suggested that discoveries in basic science led to industrial technological development. Thus, for Schumpeter, the supply of new technologies is more important than the adaptation to market demand. Knight (1963), who studied innovations in the evolution of computers between 1944 and 1962, found that manufacturers rather than users (market), dominated innovation in computers. Similarly, Berger (quoted by Betz, 1987), who examined innovation in scientific instruments and in plastics, discovered that most innovations were generated by manufacturers rather than markets. This style of innovation is characterised by 'professional Research and Development (R&D) departments within the firm, employment of qualified scientists as well as engineers within scientific training both in research and other technical functions in the firm, and acceptance of science-based technological change as a way of life for the firm'.

To be successful on the basis of this Technology-Push theory, the firm requires mainly to keep in contact with developments in basic science and to maintain a substantial technological development capability. The basic premise underlying the model is that innovation is significantly connected to R&D activities. As Rothwell (1986) argues, this model implies a more or less passive role for the user. Thus, the Technology-Push model suggests that developing countries, whose technological resources are very limited, have insufficient access to innovation and economic development.

For the demand-led model (Need-Pull), innovation arises in response to the recognition of a perceived market need. Unlike the Technology-Push model, the Need-Pull model focuses on the user as the starting point of the whole process of innovation. Studies have begun to place considerable emphasis on the role and importance of the marketplace as the main basis for innovation and technological change. For instance, Enos' study (1958) of process innovation in the petroleum industry, Freeman's work on the chemical industry (1967), Lionetta's research on the pultrusion industry, quoted by Betz (1987), and Eric Von Hippel's studies (1976) of the scientific instrumentation industry, and of the semiconductor and electronic subassembly manufacturing sector (1977), have produced similar results in that users, or demand from the market, were more often the cause of innovation rather than the manufacturers.

The debate about whether Technology-Push is distinguishable from Need-Pull and if so, which is more important, was somewhat protracted and had no very clear outcome. Studies such as Carter and Williams (1957), Langrish *et al.* (1972), Gibbons and Johnston (1974), SAPPHO (1974), Rothwell (1977) and others suggest that demand (Need-Pull) is the most important determinant of the innovation process. Specifically, Bessant and Grunt (1985) believe that Need-Pull is more important than Technology-Push for manufacturing innovations.

Similarly, Langrish *et al.* (1972) and Georghiou *et al.* (1986) argue that very few innovations resulted from a previous scientific discovery. Most of the innovation process studies found no significance in the relationship between innovation and scientific activities. R&D, whose major task is to ensure that new products are available when required, is regarded by Rothwell (1992) and Freeman (1996) as playing an important role but not being the only generator of innovation.

It seems, therefore, difficult to opt for a simple model classification because of the interaction which occurs within the innovative activity between the marketing and the scientific activities. The speed with which advances emerge is often considered as depending on the importance of R&D (e.g. the number of qualified R&D personnel and technical facilities). Hence, Landes (1986) in his historical study of technology in the West could argue that '...man can now order technological and scientific advances as one can order a commodity'. Consequently, it has a major significance in organisations' marketing strategy, since it assists them in generating new markets and in competing efficiently. Such a position of strength within a market can, as argued by economists such as Schumpeter, encourage innovation. The causation is seen to run from market power to innovation, although Millers and Sawers in their investigation into the technical development of aircraft concluded that market dominance impedes innovation whereas competition stimulates innovation. In fact, and as Utterback *et al.* (1973) suggest, in most cases ideas for innovation originate with identification of a need followed by a search for technical possibilities to meet that need. There is therefore quite often a connection between a perceived need where marketing has a considerable role to play and a technological development based essentially on efficient R&D activities.

From the 1970s onward, these two models were criticised for not taking into consideration the complexity of innovation and the interactions of different key influential factors (Von Hippel, 1988; Walsh *et al.*, 1992; Tidd *et al.*, 1997).

2.2. Theory Based on a Conjunction of Technology-Push and Need-Pull: the Coupling Model

Mowery and Rosenberg (1979) assert that both a knowledge base of science and technology and the market are important determinants of success in innovation. They discount any particular factor as the sole or the fundamental determinant of innovation and claim that the coupling of technology and the market is essential if an innovation is to be successful. This is why Pavitt (1984b, 1985), Rothwell (1992) and Dodgson (1996) regard R&D as a major component, but not the sole generator of innovation. Innovation is increasingly viewed as the result of a conjunction between a perceived need and technological development. This view is convincingly supported by Tidd *et al.* (1997) for whom most of the major innovations take place as a result of the interaction of technology, science and market. As suggested by Freeman (1974), it involves 'a synthesis of some kind of need with some kind of technical possibility'. This combination is contingent on the type and nature of innovation. The role of R&D is, for instance, more important when the innovation is a radical one. It could therefore be assumed that firms without R&D facilities, such as the majority of organisations from developing countries, are most likely to be involved chiefly in innovative activity of the incremental type.

This debate was also refined by the findings of the Queen's Award study (Langrish *et al.*, 1972) which proposed the following complex classification of models of innovation.

i.   Science Discovers Technology Applies.
ii.   Technology Discovers.
iii.   Customer Need.
iv.   Management by Objectives.

However, the authors of the Post-Innovation Performance Study suggested that very few of the innovations studied fitted these models in 'a clear and unambiguous way' (Georghiou *et al.*, 1986). It was instead found that the motives for innovation were stemmed from a combination of factors rather than a single one. This was also confirmed by the SAPPHO project (1974), Bessant and Grunt's studies on manufacturing innovations (1985) and others. In this context, the SAPPHO study, undertaken by the Science Policy Research Unit (SPRU) of Sussex University, has strongly rejected the 'single factors' explanation of the innovation process in favour of the multi-factor approach.

2.3. Integrated Model

The above studies have shown that innovation is very complex and needs to be described in terms of a multi-factor approach. It is not possible to consider either 'need' or 'science' to be the sole or the fundamental determinant of innovation. This argument, which goes far beyond the crude dichotomies discussed in the debate on the 'Technology Push' versus 'Need-Pull' theories, has been advanced by works such as that of Dosi (1982, 1984), Freeman *et al.* (1982), Nelson and Winter (1982), Clark and Juma (1987) and Freeman and Perez (1988), Nelson (1992), Rothwell (1992, 1996), Freeman (1996) and Tidd *et al.*(1997).

Freeman and his colleagues claim that neither Technology-Push nor Demand-Pull is found to be predominant significantly. Nelson and Winter (1982) explain the innovation process in terms of the interactions between an organisation's natural trajectory and the selection environment. The ability of an organisation to innovate is determined by market environments which are viewed as the basis of natural selection. Thus, in addition to the interaction of Technology-Push and Need-Pull, Nelson and Winter's theory introduces the concepts of natural trajectory and selection environment. They further explain that differences in innovative capabilities of organisations largely arise 'from differences in their institutional behaviour and strategy'.

Similarly, Dosi (1982) argues that innovation is a cumulative process of iteration between technical feasibilities and market possibilities. For Freeman and Perez (1988), the interaction is not limited merely to market and technology but also affects the economic, social and institutional context in order to determine the best practice pattern for innovation. This concept of interaction has also been expanded by Clark and Juma (1987) who, in their case study, suggest that innovation is the outcome of the cumulative scientific and technical know-how and the organisations' expenditures on R&D. As already explained previously, these authors assert that innovation also depends on feedback mechanisms between external environments and technical developments provided by institutions.

2.4. Systems Integration and Networking Model

Rothwell (1992) claims in his historical study of technological change that the present model of innovation is significantly and increasingly being influenced by the formation of networks, collaboration and alliances leading to a variety of external relationships. He calls this model a fifth-generation model marked by systems integration and networking.

As already described, models such as Technological Paradigms (Dosi), Natural Trajectories (Nelson and Winter), Cluster of Innovations (Mensch) and Long Cycles of Innovations of the World Economy (Freeman), Techno-economic Paradigm (Freeman and Perez), Organic Approach (Clark and Juma) and Systems Integration and Networking (Rothwell, 1992) have essentially been developed for the following reasons.

i.   To contribute to the understanding of the innovation process characterised by various interactions and mechanisms.
ii.   To provide a more realistic and accurate representation of the innovation process.
iii. To help implement and effectively manage innovation.

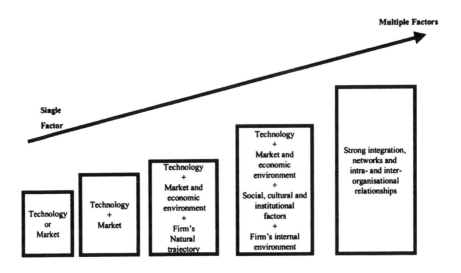

Figure 1.1: Different models of innovation.
Source: M. Saad (1991)

Innovation has to be defined as an interaction of the dynamics of the process, the firm and the environment in which the firm operates. It is therefore a phenomenon which escapes the neo-classical assumption of perfect information inasmuch as it creates more uncertainty and more information and depends on a multi-factor analysis as illustrated in Figure 1.1.

As a consequence of the complexity and the numerous interactions existing within the innovation process, research on innovation as summarised in Table 1.1, has not yet been able to describe entirely how innovation works in real life. For Ray and Uhlmann (1979), the results of the research on innovation were too fragmentary and did not provide an explanation of the whole system. Coombs *et al.* (1987) argued that there was still the possibility of a 'residual' degree of indeterminacy in innovative behaviour which was marked by uncertainty.

3. Nature of the Innovative Activity

Innovation is not a single nor an instantaneous act but a whole sequence of events that occurs over time and which involves all the activities of bringing a new product or process to the market. Rickards (1985) views innovation as 'any thought, behaviour or thing that is new'. However, the scope of interaction and complexity of innovation may be better indicated by the work of Bigoness and Perreault (1981) quoted in the National Science Foundation's report (May, 1983) and Rothwell (1992) for whom innovation is an 'interplay of products, processes and related human behaviour'. It is also worth adding that Rickards considers innovation as a 'system dealing with two subsystems'. The first subsystem concerns the firm and its capacity to deal with innovation. The

Models	Authors	Major contributions
Technology Push	Schumpeter	Economic growth is achieved by introduction of new idea where science and technology are the major sources of innovation
Clusters of innovation	Mensch	Stalemate creates an accelerator mechanism and induces innovation which comes in clusters
Need-Pull	Schmookler	Innovation is the result of emphasis put on demand factors
Coupling model	Mowery and Rosenberg	Technology and demand are both determinants of success in innovation
Long cycles of the world economy	C. Freeman	Electronics industries considered to form the basis of a fourth Kondratiev wave with innovation arising in the upswing phase as an outcome of both market and technology
Natural trajectories	Nelson and Winter	Innovation is viewed as an interaction between the firm's natural trajectory and the selection environment
Technological paradigm	Dosi	Technological paradigm incorporates inter-relationships between scientific progress, technical change and economic development and suggests a continuous progress along a defined technological trajectory
Social and economic paradigm	Freeman and Perez	Innovation is viewed as an economic interaction between the economic social and institutional spheres
Organic	Clark and Juma	Innovation is an evolutionary process cumulative through time within a social system where institutions provide feedback mechanisms between external environments and technical development
Regional network paradigm	Porter, Kanter Camgni, Cooke and Morgan	Significant links between innovation and regional support and learning
Systems integration and network paradigm	Rothwell	Innovation as a multi-factor process depending on intra- and inter-organisational relationships

Table 1.1: Major models of innovation

second is inherent in the external environment characterised by technological, economic, social and institutional factors.

Like technology transfer, the term innovation is broadly defined in this book as new ideas which can lead to enhanced performance. Both concepts seek chiefly the implementation of new ideas and are regarded as a complex sequence of events involving many different functions, actors and variables and forming a process which is not reducible to simple factors. Tidd *et al.* (1997) claim that failing to secure an understanding of the process of innovation as a whole can lead to one-factor analysis based solely on one of the many important aspects of the process.

Similar to technology transfer, innovative activity is relevant to disciplines as diverse as engineering, anthropology, sociology, psychology, organisation theory, economics and political science. Each discipline scrutinises the innovation process according to its own interests.

For economists, innovation is viewed as a vital factor in fostering economic growth. Schumpeter's work for instance emphasised the importance of innovation as a means of stimulating economic growth and the key agent of change was the entrepreneur. Work by Solow (1957) and Kendricks (1984) in separate studies, has shown that over the period 1890 to 1960 technological advance has been responsible for 55% to 70% of increases in output. Similarly Peck and Otto's work on Japan showed that between 1953 and 1971 technical change was responsible for more than 20% of the total increase in Japan's national income. Enos (1958) reported that technical improvements in refinery technology in the US oil industry had led to the following result:

i.   the unit capacity of oil refineries increased from 90 barrels a day to more than 36,000 barrels a day;
ii.   98% saving in labour costs;
iii.   80% saving in the use of capital;
iv.   50% saving in the use of material input.

Studies by economists ranging from Kondratiev to Freeman *et al.* (1982) suggest clearly that, by raising the productivity of labour, capital, land and other natural resources, innovation has had a dominant role in stimulating long-term growth.

Although economists have not explored the dynamics of a stage model, they have, however, taken into account dynamic change over time and have developed techniques such as econometrics for analysing time-series data.

For psychologists and specialists of organisational behaviour, innovation in organisation in terms of enhanced performance is mostly perceived as team effort and the aim is to understand changes in human behaviour. Various studies have been made as to the dynamics of groups (Tuckman,1965; Jewel and Reitz,1981; McGrath, 1984); motivation (Herzberg *et al*,1959; and others); leadership (Kahn and Katz, 1960; Fiedler's Contingency Theory of leadership), and communication (Simpson,1959; Berlo,1960). For Zaltman *et al.* (1973), the objective of these studies was to define any idea about how the organisational behaviour of members could be changed in order to improve the performance of the organisation. Indeed various studies on the use of new technology in industrialised countries (Fleck,1983; Nicholas *et al.*, 1983) have highlighted the need for consultation and early involvement so that resistance to implementation of innovation can be avoided.

Sociologists and organisation theorists also focus on human behaviour but only on that part which involves interaction among people in groups or organisations. They are concerned with the internal structure of the group rather than with interpersonal influences. Their objective is to look at the concept of structure, its major dimensions and its implications for individual and for collective behaviour in order to define the best way for organisations to implement innovation. Woodward (1965), Burns and Stalker (1966) and Trist (1981) focused on patterns of organisational adaptations and showed that the best structure for an organisation dealing with innovation is a structure which matches the environment. A similar conclusion was reached by Lawrence and Lorsch (1967) who suggested that 'fast changing environments require highly differentiated structures accompanied by integrating mechanisms to assist communication between departments'. Child (1977) proposed an approach contingent upon each specific situation. Indeed, innovation requires appropriate organisational structures. The traditional and increasingly inappropriate model based on mass production and bureaucratic procedures is too rigid to respond to changes brought about by advanced technology.

Political sciences focus on the pursuit of interests through the formation of groups and the distribution of interests. They centre on issues such as the impact of government decisions, decision-making methods and the politics of implementation. Decision processes play an important role in innovation. Decision-makers in the organisation are faced with choices to innovate or not, to select from different innovations and to use different methods of implementation. In addition, Lawrence and Lorsch (1967) and Schon (1967) emphasised the importance of the risk and uncertainty element that the decision-makers may experience.

For engineers, the primary concern is the production process. Individuals and groups are seen as components to be integrated with mechanical parts into that process. They focus on the efficiency of the various means for achieving production. They are, therefore, more involved with the implementation of innovation directly relevant to production. For the authors of the National Science Foundation's report (1983) and Fransman (1986), these models of implementation tend to be rather 'atomistic' and 'reductionist' in the treatment of human and social relationships.

The involvement of each of these fields is necessary but none of them can by itself enable the firm to assimilate and control such a complex and multidimensional process. As illustrated in Figure 1.2, a comprehensive study of innovation needs to be based on a multidisciplinary approach using each discipline's input in a complementary way.

Innovation is therefore systemic since it always needs to be linked with economic, psychological, social, political and technical aspects of the environment and it involves various communities of interests. There is, therefore, a need to opt for a holistic approach which takes into consideration the goals, objectives and methods of each subsystem as well as the whole system.

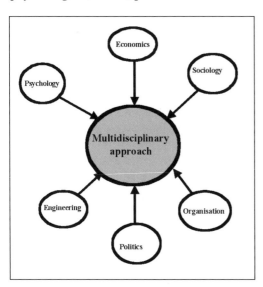

Figure 1.2: The study of innovation

4. Process of Innovation

The complexity of innovation makes difficult any attempt to describe this process. This is why most studies of innovation and technology transfer have utilised the concept of activities occurring in stages or phases. The main objective of this section is to identify these key stages in order to examine the effective management of innovation in the context of developing countries.

4.1 The Concept of Stage in the Process of Innovation

Zaltman *et al.* (1973) explain that innovation is 'composed of a set of stages or phases'. For Cooper (1980), stages are 'one or more decisions and related behaviours which are concerned in some logical fashion and which move the process toward subsequent decisions'. Innovative activity is therefore examined as a process constituted of a series of decisions and actions taken at different times with respect to choice and implementation of a new idea.

This concept of stage is therefore utilised as a way of organising the process of innovation which is considered as being long, complex, dynamic and showing interaction and overlap between its elements (see Figure 1.3). It is, however, worth emphasising that dividing the innovation process into delimited stages may represent a rationalisation rather than reality, particularly if the progression through the stages is

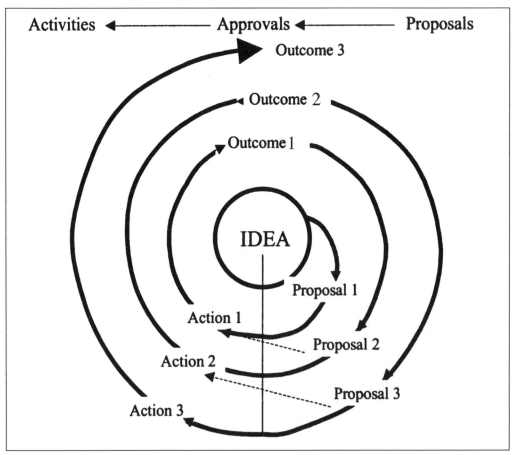

Figure 1.3: Rosegger's model of innovation
Source: Rosegger (1980) 'The Economics of Production and Innovation', Pergamon Press, London.

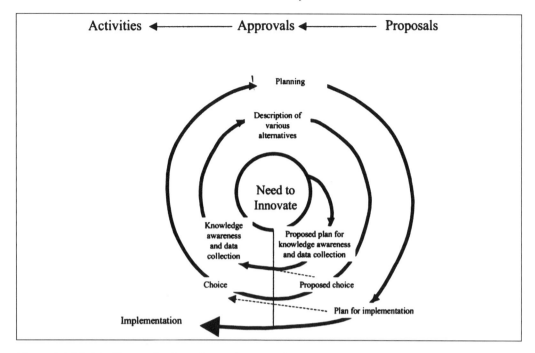

Activities ◄─────── Approvals ◄─────── Proposals

Planning

Description of
various
alternatives

Need to
Innovate

Knowledge
awareness
and data
collection

Proposed plan for
knowledge awareness
and data collection

Choice

Proposed choice

Plan for implementation

Implementation

Figure 1.4: Model of innovation from the user's perspective.
Source: Derived from Rosegger (1980) 'The Economics of Production and Innovation', Pergamon Press, London.

supposed to be linear. This implies that each stage will be clearly identifiable, whereas in practice, the boundaries between stages are usually blurred, and their order may vary. It also assumes that the process has a clear start and that activities are equally distributed among the different stages. Such assumptions are strongly rejected by the literature. Cooper (op. cit.), who found it difficult to generalise about the order in which the process works, argues that linear progression in innovation contradicts historical facts, even as early as the industrial revolution. As Rosegger (1980) argues, the linear process does not take into account the numerous and complicated feed-back mechanisms influencing the process of innovation. In practice, and as illustrated by studies such as Lambright (1980) and Pelz (1980), the linear progression model fails to account for the way in which decisions affect each other within the process of innovation.

As a solution Rosegger (1980) proposes a model (Figure 1.3), based not on stages, but on a multi-cycle search for

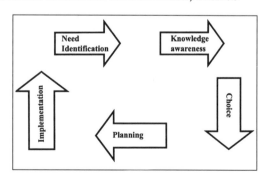

Figure 1.5: Main stages of the process of innovation

information in which decision-makers can return a new idea to a previous cycle, terminate it at any level of development, speed it up or slow it down depending on the existing circumstances. They can also modify the orientation in response to change dictated by or feedback from the internal and external environment of the firm. Rosegger's suggestion appears to match with the theories that suggest innovation is dynamic and depends on interactions and feedback mechanisms with internal and external environment.

Rosegger's representation, however, addressed innovation from the point of view of the producer of technology. As the outstanding concern for this book is to examine how technology is transferred, implemented and used by organisations from developing countries, a model representing and describing innovation from the user's point of view is proposed in Figure 1.4.

4.2. Key Stages in the Process of Innovation

As a result of the complexity and the dynamic nature of the innovation process involving multiple interactions of many actors at different levels, inside and outside the organisation, it is extremely difficult to build up a model illustrating exactly and entirely such activities. For ease of description, and in order to reflect this complexity of innovation and technology transfer in developing countries, this new model proposes a model divided into five major stages namely (Figure 1.5): identification of the need to innovate; knowledge awareness; choice; planning and implementation. This choice has been motivated by the necessity for acquiring an in-depth understanding of the mechanisms by which key stages of innovation and technology transfer can effectively be shaped and managed.

Rogers	Nabseth and Ray	Bessant	Zaltman
1.Relative advantage	1.Technical applicability	1.Complexity	1.Cost
2.Compatibility	2.Profitability	2.Compatibility	2.Return on investment
3.Complexity	3.Finance	3.Champion	3.Efficiency
4.Triability	4.Size		4.Risk and uncertainty
5.Observability	5.Structure		5.Communicability
	6.Organisation		6.Compatibility
	7.Management attitude		7.Complexity
	8.R&D activities		8.Scientific status
	9.Access		9.Relative advantage
	to information		10.Point of origin
			11.Terminality
			12. Commitment
			13. 'Publicness' versus 'privateness'
			14.Gatekeepers
			15.Susceptibility to successive modifications
			16.Gateway capacity

Table 1.2: Summary of key attributes

Stage 1: Identification of the Need to Innovate

In this stage, a need for change is identified and defined. However, and as mentioned in the debate on Technology-Push and Demand-Pull, the question of whether an awareness of a need or an awareness of an innovation comes first, has so far not been answered. This, as argued by Bessant and Grunt (1985), clearly shows that the need to innovate rarely occurs as a result of a single motive but rather as an aftermath of diverse concurrent motives. Consequently there must be strong interaction and feedback mechanisms between need identification, awareness and factors such as the national system of innovation and the economic, social and cultural environment. This will minimise the risk of making an incorrect decision.

Stage 2: Developing Awareness

This stage includes data collection in order to understand and enable a greater awareness of the new idea with the overall aim of minimising difficulties of implementation and ensuring success. It starts when the first information on a new idea enters the organisation. The objective is basically to acquire knowledge and understanding of the functioning principles of the new idea or device to increase expertise. Data collection and training are essentially based upon scientific, technical, and research activities. If an adequate level of information and understanding are not gained, other stages are likely to be affected. If, for instance, an incorrect decision is made there will be an incompatibility between the new idea or the new technology and the host environment.

Stage 3: Selecting the Innovation

Subsequent systematic evaluation then leads to a decision to adopt or reject a new process or idea having fully considered all problems likely to occur during the implementation phase. In this stage, the major aim is to collect the data necessary to explore the strengths and the weaknesses of the innovation in order to determine how best it can be successfully introduced into a given situation. Alternative innovations are listed, evaluated and compared on the basis of their main characteristics. A summary of influential characteristics proposed by Zaltman (1973), Nabseth and Ray (1974), Bessant (1982) and Rogers (1983) is presented in Table 1.2.

From this review of key attributes to examine prior to any selection or adoption of innovation, it can be argued that the most influential factors to take into account are relative advantage, compatibility, complexity and key individuals.

i. Relative Advantage

Rogers defines relative advantage as 'the degree to which an innovation is perceived as better than the idea it supersedes'. The degree of relative advantage is measured in economic terms such as reduction of production cost, productivity increase, saving in time and effort and immediacy of the reward. The greater the perceived relative advantage of an innovation, the more rapid and successful its rate of adoption.

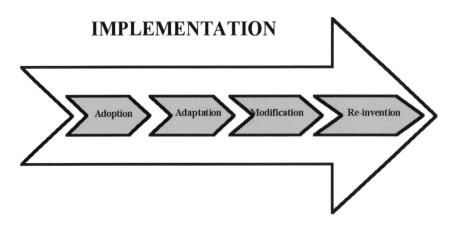

Figure 1.6: Implementation stage.

ii. Compatibility

For Rogers and Schoemaker (1971), compatibility is 'the degree to which an innovation is perceived as consistent with existing values, past experiences and needs of the receivers'. It concerns the 'fit' between innovation and the context in which it is going to be implemented.

iii. Complexity

Rogers (1983) views complexity as 'the degree to which an innovation is perceived as difficult to understand and use'. A new idea which is simple to understand will be adopted rapidly. A more complex innovation which requires new skills and understanding may lead to complex implementation and increased risk and uncertainty.

Jaikumar and Bohn (1986) report that complexity and compatibility take the form of 'misalignments' between the technology and (a) local requirements, and (b) the system through which the technology is delivered to users.

iv. Key Individuals

Key individuals are those responsible for identifying and disseminating information about technological opportunities.

The identification and dissemination of relevant information is examined in order to select the most suitable alternative. Adoption is decided at this level. This is not yet the end of the innovation process as this idea now has to be implemented. Adoption is only the final step of the conceptual activity based upon information gathering and processing.

Stage 4: Planning

This stage represents a transition between the conceptual activities and the implementation. The major objective of this stage is to anticipate events which are likely to occur in order to ensure the best fit between innovation and the context in which it is going to be operated. Once this step is completed, the innovation is ready to be put into practice.

Stage 5: Implementing

This phase is increasingly seen as the heart of the innovation process as successful innovation is often associated with effective implementation (Voss, 1996). Implementation is the part of the process that leads to the successful adoption of the innovation and in which the user or the recipient of the technology is supposed to be actively involved.

Implementing an innovation is getting it 'up and running' in daily operations. In the case of technology transfer, implementation encompasses the actions from purchase and installation through to the successful use of the technology. It includes activities such as acquisition of new equipment, the undertaking of associated construction work, the equipment installation, consultation, training, cost control, commissioning, and hand-over. It also includes actions prior to purchase and installation such as strategic planning, technical planning and workforce consultation.

The process of implementation has its roots in the organisation's background and history, and includes both pre-installation as well as post-installation factors (Voss, 1996). It is a prolonged process entailing progressive development, evaluation, adaptation and co-operative relationships with technology suppliers (Rhodes and Wield, 1985). Consequently, implementation is not simply about adopting an innovation as advocated by the classical diffusion literature (Roger and Schoemaker, 1971). It is clearly a process which does end with the assumption of adoption. It is a continuous development process putting decisions into actions with a significant reflection of the very considerable obstacles that may have to be overcome. As suggested by Bessant (1990), implementation is a continuous problem-solving process with a long time- scale and many dimensions.

The importance of on-going change featuring implementation is also highlighted by Leonard-Barton (1988) who depicts this stage as a dynamic process of mutual adaptation, between the innovation and its environment. Effective implementation is also significantly associated with the implementation 'champion', incremental stepwise installation, workforce engagement, relations to technology vendors, training and cross-functional implementation teams (Leonard-Barton, 1991; Winch and Voss, 1991). Implementation is a long, complex and dynamic process with many dimensions. Empirical studies have shown that in spite of all the conceptual work completed in the previous stages to reduce uncertainty and the risk of failure, risks associated with implementation cannot be entirely eliminated.

Effective management of the post-adoption consolidation phase can be crucial in sustaining effective implementation. At this stage, and as a result of learning and experience, the innovation must be reviewed and modified in order to match it with the requirements of the organisation and its environment. These activities have been variously termed: routinisation, incorporation, stabilisation or continuation (Zaltman *et al.*, 1973; Lambright, 1980). The consolidation stage includes adaptation, modification and sometimes re-invention. These activities acknowledge the dynamic aspect of innovation and the importance of interaction between the different factors which may affect its successful implementation. The overall aim is to sustain an appropriate level of compatibility between the innovation and its environment.

i. Adaptation

> The adaptation activity brings about changes to the innovation to ensure success and reduce any incompatibility with the environment. The adaptation process is even more necessary in developing countries because a technology almost never fits perfectly into the user environment. Adaptation may cause change to the organisation too. Indeed Van de Ven, quoted by Leonard-Barton (1988) claims that 'innovations not only adapt to existing organisational and industrial arrangements, but they also transform the structure and practice of these environments'.

ii. Modification

> As a result of development activities, training and learning, the organisation undertakes alterations to the technology used in order to improve and sustain its performance. Zaltman *et al*. (1973) consider this process as 'forces altering the innovation'.

iii. Reinvention

> This is an activity whose sole purpose is to renew the innovation according to the context in which it is operated or used. It is described by Rice and Rogers (1980) as an alteration of the original innovation to suit users' needs. For Johnson and Rice (1987) the reinvention phase is important when the innovation is used in ways unforeseen by the original developers. At this step, the organisation is likely to be in possession of a level of research and experience which encourages them to undertake substantial changes to the innovation.

Implementation, the major stage of the innovation process, relies significantly upon the conceptual work undertaken in the previous stages. Organisational learning and problem-solving, which are for instance the basis of post-adoption activities, can be facilitated by accurate conceptual work. Although implementation is separated from the pre-adoption stages, in reality they are closely linked. Successful implementation is therefore the outcome of:

i.   accurate and adequate conceptual work;
ii.   greater interaction with other stages of the innovation process;
iii.   early involvement of the user;
iv.   continuous and organisational learning;
v.   a systemic approach;
vi.   a multidiscipline approach;
vii.   managing implementation in an integrated way.

Innovation success or failure is influenced by a whole range of factors which may vary from one organisation to another, from one industry to another, and from one country to another.

Projects	Major contributions	Limitations
Carter and Williams	Innovation impeded by paucity of marketing	1. Studies based essentially on factors related to success.
Myers and Marquis	1. Innovation results more frequently from marketing than form technical activity 2. Innovation arising from marketing was more frequent in small companies and innovation from technical factors was more frequent in larger companies	2. Studies based on generalisations. The specificity of firms, industries and countries are not taken into account. 3. Innovation is perceived as ending with adoption
Rogers	Innovation is successful when it is perceived as being compatible and not bringing a relative advantage	
Queen's Award Study	1. Factors of success include clear identification of a need, a top person, good co-operation, availability of resources and help from government 2. Factors of failure include no market or need, poor communication, shortage of resources, resistance to new ideas.	
SAPPHO	1. No single factor explanation 2. Factors of success include marketing activity, good internal and external communication and co-operation, top management commitment. 3. Factors of failure include ignorance of user' needs, paucity of marketing, lack of effective management and communication	The idea of generalisation still exist and the emphasis is put on the producer's side of innovation.
Freeman	Factors of success include strong in-house professional R&D, performance of basic research, readiness to take risks, identification of a need and market research, good internal and external communication.	The study concerns essentially organisations in developed countries.
Brusco Beccatini Porter Camgini Kanter Cooke and Morgan	Factors of success include regional support and network for learning and innovation	The study concerns essentially industries and organisations in developed countries.

Table 1.3: Major studies of success and failures of innovation

5. Influential Factors in Success and Failure of Innovation

Several key characteristics of successful and unsuccessful innovations have been suggested by empirical work. Different studies highlight different factors but, as Swords-Isherwood (1984) and Tidd *et al.* (1997) explain, when a number of studies are considered together, there seems to be strong evidence to suggest that not only are these individual factors important in innovation but also combinations of particular factors are also necessary for success. The major empirical studies are outlined in Table 1.3.

The study carried out by Carter and Williams (1957) was the first systematic data analysis concerning the factors involved in the initiation of commercial innovation. Teubal *et al.* (1976) followed with their FIP study (the Falk Innovation Project) and observed the lack of market appraisal and marketing research in British organisations. Swords-Isherwood, (1984) analysing this work, explains that explicit consideration of market demand factors was rare in decisions concerning the level of investment in R&D in British organisations.

Myers and Marquis (1969) in their study of successful innovation suggested that innovation is not a single action but a total process. They found that innovation arising from market factors was more frequent in small companies while innovation arising from technical or production factors was more frequent in large companies. Recognition of demand was seen as a more frequent factor in innovation than recognition of technical potential. For Myers and Marquis the success of innovation was the result of more emphasis being placed on market research.

The research completed by Langrish *et al.* (1972) covered 84 firms and incidentally gained the Queen's Award to Industry for innovation between 1966 and 1969. It also came to the conclusion that clear identification of a need was a major factor associated with success. The lack of marketing activity was identified by the authors of this study as a factor causing delay in innovation.

The SAPPHO (1974) analysis, undertaken by the Science Policy Research Unit of Sussex University, was a comparative analysis between successful and unsuccessful innovation in the chemical and scientific instrument industries. The findings of this project strongly confirm the hypothesis of Langrish *et al* (1972), Carter and Williams (1957) and other works in the field, that the use of marketing and the identification of user needs clearly influence the success or failure of innovation. In line with these studies, the SAPPHO project also suggests that success in innovative activity requires competence, experience and effective communication. Failure on the other hand was caused by the ignorance of user requirements and the lack of market research. Most of the above studies also agreed with the importance of the R&D's task of discovering up the best way to satisfy the identified needs.

The SAPPHO project was designed to observe and study innovations which succeed as well as those which fail. Most of the studies on influential factors, summarised in Table 1.3, have mainly been based on factors related to success, as these have been more easily identified and observed than the unsuccessful ones. These studies were also developed on the assumption that the identification of features correlated with success would systematically lead to the converse correlation being associated with failure. Hence the general belief that factors associated with a successful innovation can easily be implemented by other firms regardless of the dissimilarities which may exist. However, this idea of generalisation doe not correspond to reality, especially to organisations in developing countries. Nelson and Winter (1982) suggested that each firm has its natural trajectory and selection environment and it is therefore quite risky to generalise about determinants of innovation which are contingent on their environment, location and national systems of innovation (Porter, 1995; Lundvall, 1990; Cooke and Morgan, 1993 and Nelson, 1993). Consequently, success or failure of innovation is caused by a combination of factors which varies from one situation to another.

Despite the heterogeneity of approach and content of the projects outlined above, a number of common factors have emerged as characterising successful innovators. For instance, understanding user needs, good communication and effective collaboration tend to be strongly associated with success. The lack of these factors is identified with failure.

For Rothwell (1977, 1988, 1992, 96) and Tidd *et al.* (1997) the major factors are as follows:

i.   the achievement of good internal and external linkages;
ii.   treating innovation as a corporate-wide task;
iii.   taking a strategic approach;
iv   implementing effective planning and project control procedures;
v.   efficiency in development work and high quality production;
vi.   developing and sustaining a supporting organisational context for innovation;
vii.   presence of certain key individuals and quality management;
viii. top management commitment and acceptance of risk;
ix.   corporate flexibility and responsiveness to change;
x.   effective and on-going learning process.

Consequently, success is rarely associated with doing one or two things outstandingly, but rather with performing all functions competently and in a well balanced and integrated manner. Despite the numerous empirical studies carried out to determine the factors associated with success and failure in innovation and despite the similarities of their outcomes, there still exists no precise or easy 'prescription' or 'recipe' for successful innovation.

In addition, most of these concepts have been developed essentially for advanced economies and bears little reference to the specific mode of development in developing countries. It can therefore be assumed that the degree of uncertainty of innovation identified by this literature review is even higher in developing countries.

Note

1. The main learning approaches are examined in Chapter 8.

Chapter 2
Technology Transfer and Development

This chapter proposes to lay out a conceptual framework, through definitions, theoretical discussion and a review of the relevant literature of technology transfer in developing countries. It also uses the theory of innovation, reviewed in the previous chapter, as a basis to scrutinise the critical elements of technology transfer affecting its implementation, control and management from the recipient or user's perspective.

Technology transfer as a separate field, did not appear until the 1970s. It emerged as a result of accelerating awareness of the key role of technology in economic development and its study has essentially been driven by the need to better understand the process, its determinants, its effects on transferor and transferee and factors affecting its control. Most of the research on technology transfer can be divided into two main groups. The first has essentially investigated issues such as the appropriateness and effectiveness of the technology transferred to developing countries, while research in the second group has focused on topics relevant to the technology supplier such as strategic management and corporate policy.

Although this book focuses on technology transfer in developing countries from the perspective of the recipient or user, it will also highlight the crucial need for taking into consideration all the factors, interactions and feedback which constitute the process of technology transfer. It is therefore unlikely to achieve a comprehensive study of technology transfer through a single-factor analysis.

Like innovation, technology transfer is a lengthy, complex and dynamic process which is affected and shaped by interactions between various factors originating from many different sources. It has been defined in a variety of ways, allocated different objectives and has been undertaken through various mechanisms. It is thought of as being product-embodied, process-embodied, or personnel-embodied (Chen, 1996). Hoffman and Girvan (1990) suggest that technology transfer in developing countries needs to be perceived in terms of achieving the following three core objectives:

i.   the introduction of new techniques by means of investment of new plants;
ii.   improvement of existing techniques;
iii. the generation of new knowledge.

Technology transfer has also been described as a process based on a movement of technology from one place to another which can be either from one organisation to another, or from a university to an organisation or from one country to another (Schon, 1967; Solo and Rogers, 1972). This process encompasses two concepts: technology and transfer, which are both difficult to define in a clear manner.

Technology in itself is complex. It consists of many dimensions such as hardware (Woodward, 1965), search procedures (Perrow, 1967) or skill and knowledge (Rousseau *et al.*, 1984). The intricacy of technology is related to its diversity of forms ranging from a simple technical process to a very complex electronic or computer system. Fransman

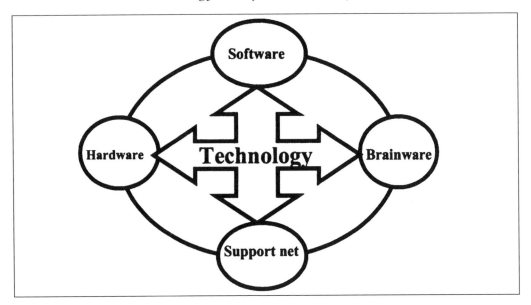

Figure 2.1: The main components of technology

(1984) on the other hand refers to technology as activities involved in transforming inputs into outputs. This definition, in terms of production and technical, is also echoed by Stewart and Nihei (1987) who regard technology as an innovation which is associated with new and better ways of achieving economic growth and development. Technology is also delineated in terms of knowledge and skills necessary for a specific task, such as utilising a production technique or making a specific product. Technology is therefore a whole range of knowledge, skills, ideas, equipment, and facilities that organisations need to produce goods and services. It is a blending of 'hardware', 'software', 'brainware' and 'support net' as illustrated in Figure 2.1 .

'Hardware' is merely related to the physical equipment, structure of components and layout. Software is about the 'know-how' needed for accomplishing a specific task . 'Brainware' is more intricate as it includes the necessary knowledge and understanding related to the application and justification of hardware and software deployment. It is also known as the 'know-what' and 'know-why' of technology. 'Support net' comprises the complex network needed to support the effective use and management of the technology. Rothwell (1992) argues in his fifth generation model of innovation based on networks and systems integration that acquisition alongside the development of 'brainware' and 'support net' (the most difficult of the four) are the most needed to ensure effective innovation and technology transfer.

Technology needs to be viewed not only as specific to the production or manufacturing process but also in terms of knowledge and experience necessary for the planning, establishment and operation of a manufacturing plant and associated enterprises. Consequently, it is critical to place a notable emphasis upon the knowledge component which includes knowledge in design, production, investment and management, areas which are largely tacit inasmuch as they are human-embodied. The most important stock of any country is not sophisticated machinery or complex equipment, but the knowledge and skills embodied in the workforce.

Technology may, therefore, be in the form of know-how, machinery or tools, technical assistance, processes, organisation or products. However, acquiring the capacity to apply, control and adapt the technology is a different issue and constitutes perhaps the key to the transfer process. If the technology embodied in the imported good is not captured by the recipient or user, technology transfer will never happen.

The debate on the meaning, objectives and mechanisms of transfer is also far from being settled. Mansfield (1968) distinguishes three types of transfer that can be associated with the main elements of technology as shown in the Figure 2.1. The first consists of the transfer of materials, final products, components, equipment, and even turnkey and/or product-in-hand plants. The second form of transfer involves the movement of designs, blueprints, and the know-how. It provides the basic information, data and guidelines needed to create a desired capability. The objective of the third form of transfer is to provide know-how and software needed to adapt existing technology and innovate. This is why Fransman (1986) and Enos and Park (1988) place a greater emphasis upon the acquisition of the entire body of knowledge necessary to fulfil a specific task. This particular knowledge covers aspects such as manufacturing techniques, the design, construction and operation of plants, training and improvements.

The process of technology transfer to developing countries is increasingly being defined as the process whereby knowledge in some form changes hands from a person or organisation who possesses it to another individual or organisation (Chen, 1996).

The emphasis on the acquisition of knowledge means that technology transfer is not the same as exporting goods. The export of goods does not always imply the transfer of knowledge or the ability to apply such knowledge to a given task. However, there are instances where technology may be embodied in the actual product that is exported and if the receiver is able to capture that technology via copying or some other means, then technology transfer may indeed occur. It is also worth mentioning that such transfer does not give the recipient an ability to reproduce the knowledge but only to consume or use it.

As a result of the unsettled and controversial debate on the definition of the term 'transfer', there is some disagreement on the factors that determine whether a transfer, based on the acquisition of knowledge, has really occurred. For some, technology can be considered to be transferred only if its knowledge component is absorbed and effectively used by the transferee or user. In this case, transfer is not achieved until the transferee or user understands and can utilise and adapt the technology. For others, success in transferring technology should not be examined solely in terms of relationships between the acquired technology and the recipient's technological capabilities.[1]

The definition of transfer can be further complicated by the various channels and mechanisms through which it can occur and by the diversity of its stakeholders. This complexity is amplified by the fact that neither the process itself nor the package being

34

transferred is homogeneous. It can be transferred as a complete package, or fragmented and unpacked. The choice of the form of transfer contract is often the outcome of the recipient 's knowledge and technical capabilities and the economic, social, cultural, institutional and political environment.

Transfer can take place through a number of different channels and mechanisms including licensing; franchising, subcontracting and sale of turnkey plants. The main features of these mechanisms of and their impact on developing countries are summarised in Table 2.1 Licensing comprises a variety of contractual arrangements whereby an organisation (licensor) sells its intangible assets or property rights (patents, trade secrets, know-how, trademarks and company name) to a firm from a developing country. The transfer of these intangibles or property rights is the core of a licensing agreement. Under this arrangement, the firm provides a limited right to produce and market the product in a specified geographical region. Licensing agreements are normally long-term arrangements that may require significant investment by the licensee. The main advantages of licensing is to enable organisations to earn additional profits on existing products or technologies without making substantial new investments, either in marketing or production. It also helps licensor organisations to penetrate new markets when barriers exist. However, a major disadvantage for the licensor is the loss of control. Once a contract has been signed, the licensee from developing countries controls the manufacturing, marketing and distribution of the product. When the fear of control loss exists, licensors tend to impose restrictive terms on the licensing arrangement which can significantly hinder the transfer of technology to these developing countries. This is why Chen (1996) suggests that a successful technology transfer through licensing agreements is very dependent on co-operation, mutual commitment and trust.

Licensing can enable organisations from developing countries to get the technology to the market faster and to launch a new product without having to take the risk of spending heavily on R&D activities. However this form of agreement is often associated with high costs, lengthy negotiations and excessive adaptation and preparation before being able to utilise the licensed technology.

Franchising is a variation of licensing in which a company (franchisor) licenses an entire business system as well as offering property rights to a company from a developing country (franchisee). The franchisee organises its business under the franchisor's trade name and is expected to follow the procedures and policies established by the franchisor. This form of agreement provides the franchisor with an effective way for rapid expansion into foreign markets. However, it can mean a loss of control over the franchisee's activities. This arrangement can, for a franchisee from a developing country, constitute a relatively safe way of owning a business.

Subcontracting also known as outsourcing happens when an organisation (the principal) places an order with another organisation (the subcontractor) for the manufacture of parts, components, subassemblies, or assemblies which will be incorporated into a product that the principal will sell (UNIDO, 1975). It covers agreements ranging from the purchase of components to the complete production of specific products. Through this form of arrangement, firms from developed countries

Mechanism for technology transfer	Main Objective	Advantage to the recipient from developing countries	Disadvantage to the recipient from developing countries	Impact on technology transfer to developing countries
Licensing	Transfer of intangibles or property rights.	To get the technology to the market faster.	High costs resulting and limited impact on in-house research development capabilities. Introduction of restrictive practices to licensing agreement which can impede technology transfer.	Technology transfer which may take a long time is dependent upon appropriate local capabilities and policies and trust between licensors and licensees.
Franchising	Licensing of an entire business system as well as offer of property rights.	Safe and quick way of owning a business under an established trade name.	High cost.	Franchising is most popular in consumer service products and less with more strategic products whose manufacture requires significant capital investment and high level of managerial and technical skills.
Subcontracting	Types of agreement ranging from the purchase of components to the complete production of specific products.	Acquisition of know-how and technical assistance in areas such as plant layout, equipment selection and operation planning, training on quality management systems.	Strong dependence upon the foreign partner.	It can help develop indigenous capabilities in some major industries such as electronics and automobiles where subcontracting is important. However, transfer of technology can be limited to specific areas of subcontracting agreements. The success of transfer of technology is dependent upon the subcontracting relationship.
Turnkey	Rapid transfer of complete sets of equipment and machinery	Rapid acquisition of hardware.	Acquisition primarily limited to hardware and to learning-by-doing High cost and strong dependence on technology supplier for maintenance and operation.	Emphasis on learning-by-doing and on developing production capability.

Table 2.1: Key features of the main channels of technology transfer

can enter into new markets in developing countries without having to use significant financial and managerial resources and without losing control over their marketing activities. Companies from developing countries involved in international subcontracting can benefit from a form of technology transfer and technical assistance. The technology can be transferred in a number of ways and it can take place in both directions, either to contractor or subcontractor. For example, with a turnkey project, the technology supplier (contractor) designs, builds and installs capital investment equipment with the intention of turning over control and operation to the company from developing countries (contractor) after an agreed period. The technology supplier

Type of model	Objective of the model	Key feature to the recipient country
Hardware model	The emphasis is placed upon purchasing and acquiring of complete sets of equipment and machinery.	It can lead to a significant acceleration of technological advancement especially during the outset of the industrialising process. The acquisition is essentially undertaken through packaged contracts and may lead to a passive role of the recipient.
Software model	The priority is given to the transfer and acquisition of technological information.	It can lead to acquisition of knowledge and skills enhancing indigenous capabilities. It is a long term approach and its success requires an active involvement of the recipient through the adoption of unpackaged contracts.
Capital model	The objective is to acquire technology, management capabilities and to develop an international market through Foreign Direct Investment (FDI).	It can provide a whole set of complicated technology, management and sales techniques and sales channels. The successful acquisition of technology through this type of model is dependent upon the incentives offered to foreign investors as well as the availability of indigenous capabilities and policies aimed at capturing and maximising the benefits from such an approach.

Table 2.2: Main strategies for technology transfer

has, however, no control over distribution and sale once the original agreement has expired. This type of contract is important for the transfer of industries involving the acquisition of complex technologies and construction of large-scale capital works. However, when local capabilities are not available, this form of technology transfer often gives rise to problems with operations, repairs, maintenance and replacement as demonstrated in the selected case studies in Chapters 4 and 5.

Other approaches to technology transfer include joint ventures; co-operative research arrangements and co-production agreements; export of high-technology products and capital goods; reverse engineering; exchange of scientific and technical personnel; science and technology conferences, trade shows and exhibits; education and training; commercial visits; open literature such as journals, magazines, books and articles; industrial espionage; end-user or third-country diversions and government assistance programmes.

It is clear that the different approaches mean that different amounts of skills and knowledge will be transferred. A genuine level of information and knowledge would, for instance, enable the recipient or user to be more involved in playing a significant and active role in successfully acquiring, implementing and adapting technology by adopting a more unpacked or fragmented type of contact. Transfer can be an explicit objective as it is in the case of licensing agreements, joint ventures and training programmes. There are also cases where technology may be transferred without being received, as it is often the case of turnkey projects[2] where the technology supplier builds an entire factory using an advanced system of technology that no one in the recipient country can use or replicate. Technology can also be received without being transferred when engineers in the recipient country create a new product through reverse engineering.

The technology transfer strategies used by most developing countries can be summarised into three broad categories: hardware, software and capital models, as shown in Table 2.2. The hardware model enables developing countries acquire a significant technological capability based upon purchasing and acquiring a complete set of equipment and machinery.

With the software model, the emphasis is placed upon the transfer and the acquisition of information, knowledge and skills to allow the recipient to use, adapt and manage the technology. The aim of the capital model is to acquire, through foreign direct investment, technology and management capabilities and access to an international market.

Although much work has been done in the field of technology transfer, the reference to the theoretical framework of innovation suggests that there still exists a number of important issues which need to be investigated such as implementation and learning (Lall, 1992; Chen, 1996). Enos and Park claim that there is a scarcity of research on technology adoption, which they define as the 'entire sequence of decisions made within a developing country determining how, when, where and with what consequences technology is employed'. The importance of developing management capabilities as a prerequisite for successful technology transfer in developing countries, is also not sufficiently and adequately discussed.

Another important failure is related to the poor level of recognition for the use of a holistic and integrated approach in studying international technology transfer. This is a multi-disciplinary subject involving changes in the sociocultural, cognitive and managerial attributes of the society (Girvan and Marcell, 1900). Similar to innovation, a comprehensive study of technology transfer needs to be associated with an approach which includes not only the technical aspects of the transfer but also the related environmental factors. This necessitates viewing the process of technology transfer as a dynamic and long-term relationship between the main stakeholders.

Notes

1   The effectiveness of technology transfer and its impact on the recipient's learning curve are examined in Chapters 4, 5 and 7.
2   The key features of turnkey projects and their implications on the process of technology transfer are examined in Chapter 3.

Chapter 3
Algerian Strategy for Technology Transfer

This chapter aims to examine and assess the effectiveness of strategies for technology transfer adopted by developing countries such as Algeria which are striving to establish a significant industrial base as rapidly as possible through a programme of massive investment. The selected strategy for technology transfer has been based essentially on a combined software and hardware model (with a greater emphasis on the latter) and the use of packaged or highly integrated contracts. The acquisition of technology through the capital model or through foreign direct investment has been clearly and deliberately disregarded for ideological motives.[1] The aim of this particular technology transfer strategy was to build, as rapidly as possible, a strong industrial base and achieve a high level of technological advancement. This has required a massive programme of investment, evidenced in Algeria from 1967 to 1984, reaching a peak in the period 1967–79, followed by a downwards trend between 1980 and 1989, and a complete decline after 1990.

There is now a growing recognition that this strategy has fallen short of achieving its ambitious objectives for exploiting the full learning potential of technology transfer. Its outcomes have not at all reflected the very high level of investments. Debt has increased more rapidly than national production and wealth. The increase has even been more intensive for the debt service which has been multiplied by 30-fold between 1973 and 1993 while wealth has only been multiplied by 5.5-fold.

This failure in Algeria can be associated with the very low level of use of the available production capacity, the economic crisis with the moratorium on payments in 1993, the subsequent shift from centralised planning to market economy and the decision to restructure and privatise the loss-making public enterprises which have crippled the country's financing system.

The country is currently also undergoing a radical programme of macroeconomic stabilisation and structural reform, initiated in 1987, aimed at establishing the conditions for sustainable long-term growth and for attracting FDI. This includes correcting macroeconomic imbalances and price distortions, containing inflation, promoting private sector development, reforming and restructuring public enterprises and integrating the economy into world markets.

Until 1989, Algeria was a socialist country, its economy was centrally planned and the objectives and the strategy of economic development were set by the Central Plan. The allocation of resources and the investment programmes for the period studied here were set through four plans: 1967–69, 1970–1973, 1974–77 and 1980–84 as shown in Table 3.1.

These 'central plans' implied that the state was in charge of all decision-making procedures related to the allocation of investment among the different sectors, the financing of investment, the organisation, production, distribution and sale of goods and services.

The objectives of the central plan were to be attained by 15 national state companies which were created to cover all sectors of the economy such as petrochemical, steel, metallurgy, engineering, electronics, building materials, electrical goods, food processing, mining and textiles. These state companies were in charge of a wide range of activities including R&D, the production, distribution and sales and the import of products related to their monopoly They were seen simply as executing the strategy formulated by the central plan.

The overall aim of the central plan strategy for technological advancement and technology transfer was as follows:

i.   to master the assimilation of imported technology by 1980;
ii.   to have the necessary institutions and skills to undertake adaptations and modifications by 1985;
iii.   to be able to conduct R&D work and to become a relatively autonomous nation by the year 2000.

1. Economic Development through Rapid Industrialisation

From 1967 to 1984, the Algerian strategy was to attain economic development and growth through heavy and rapid industrialisation, this would be acquired from industrialised countries. The model of industrialisation, known as 'industrialising industries', was to be built entirely from existing natural resources of oil, iron and steel. From these other industries would grow, for instance, the petrochemical industry was to be derived from the oil industry and the metal industry from the steel industry. Through interaction and subsequent 'knock-on' effects, this would lead to the development of other key sectors of the economy as illustrated in Figure 3.1.

It was anticipated that this 'industrialising industries' model, theoretically conceived by the French economist Destanne de Bernis (1966, 1968 and 1970), would help integrate the whole economy by creating industrial and sectoral interactions and to achieve an introversion of the economy. One of the key objectives of this model was to acquire a high level of advanced technology conducive to sustainable development. It was aimed at reaching a certain level of economic growth in a relatively short period of time by acquiring advanced technology which would penetrate into the whole economy through the mechanisms of 'upstream and downstream' integration. Hveen (1978) reflecting on this Algerian experience suggested it was 'an example of an underdeveloped country attempting to profit from the international circulation of technology in a process of rapid industrialisation based on national development objectives'.

Extensive investments and resources were allocated to 'industrialisation'. These were mostly earmarked for the petrochemical, steel, mechanical, electrical and electronics industries as shown in Table 3.2.

Industry's growing need for investment often exceeded the forecasts and it consumed enormous resources to the detriment of other sectors of economic activity. Even throughout the 1980s investment in industry remained dominant in spite of its relative reduction.

41

2. Rapid Industrialisation through Transfer of Technology

To acquire and assimilate advanced technology as quickly as possible, Algerian state companies were under pressure to discount the 'capital model' of technology transfer, the acquisition of 'piece meal' technology through FDI. They were all directed to select technologies which would lead to a maximum integration of production.

This implied the purchase of complex and costly systems of technology and the use of highly integrated mechanisms of technology transfer. Unfortunately most state-owned organisations were not able to manage this effectively. This challenging but ambitious approach, driven by the need to achieve self-sufficiency as rapidly as possible, is considered as the chief cause of the ultimate failure of the Algerian strategy for technology transfer.

The desire for rapid and heavy industrialisation led in the 1970s to a significant thrust of all-embracing contracts as illustrated in Tables 3.3 and 3.4. This was made possible by the flow of 'petro-dollars' resulting form the significant rise of the oil price in 1973.

These complex and highly integrated contracts, such as turnkey and 'product-in-hand' contracts, were based upon the idea of re-assembling all the project operations and transferring the entire responsibility for activities such as conception, co-ordination and installation to the technology supplier. The concept and supporting empirical information related to these forms of contracts are extensively discussed in Waitsos (1974), Cooper and Maxwell (1975), Cooper and Hoffman (1981), Perrin (1983), and Yachir (1983). Hoffman and Girvan (1990) report that in highly packaged contracts, technology suppliers establish a quasi-monopoly over elements of technical knowledge and consequently charge a high price for the package. The decision to integrate the different project activities was mainly motivated by the need to obtain, in as short a time as possible, a plant in working order outwardly showing that technology was efficiently transferred.

Investment in key industries such as petrochemical, electronics and mechanical was all developed through integrated contracts as shown in Table 3.4.

2.1. Turnkey Contracts

Here the foreign partner takes complete responsibility for both the concept stage and the execution of the project. The technology supplier is required to deliver a plant in working order. As shown in Figure 3.2 the technology supplier is in charge of project conception, civil engineering work, machinery and process choice, delivery and installation.

However, this type of contract does not include for the sourcing or training of local skills. It therefore implies either continuing reliance on outside assistance for management and skilled operations, or an inefficient operation by local management due to a lack of understanding and skill. For these reasons, Tlemcani (1983) argues that plants transferred through turnkey contracts often face difficulties such as breakdowns, delay in spare parts deliveries and repair facilities which can only be completed by experts located abroad.

Investment	Plan
24.6% of the GNP	1967/69
46% of the GNP	1970/73
55% of the GNP	1974/79
60% of the GNP	1980/84

Table 3.1: Programme of investment from 1967 to 1984.
Source: N. Dahmani (1985).

The turnkey contract puts emphasis on acquiring hardware which is considered as being the only (and imperative) condition of technology transfer. Such an approach would probably be successful in an environment containing adequate levels of skills, experience and knowledge. However, none of these factors was available in Algeria at the time of the implementation of the first integrated contracts and as a consequence, the hardware acquired was too complex and not compatible with the local framework. Indeed, Said Amer (1978) and Tlemcani (1986) reported that the technology imported was perceived to be difficult to understand and to use and did not match with the local context.

To facilitate compatibility and to reduce complexity as much as possible, Bell (1982, 1984), Fransman (1986) and others suggest that the process of successful technology transfer needs a substantial level of 'in-house' technological capacity. However, Dahmani (1985), who, found in his investigations of 1973/74 that there were no more that 250 engineers in the whole country, argues that this requisite was not available within Algerian firms. As a consequence of this lack of local technical skill, the plants installed through the turnkey contract were found to be complex and difficult to monitor.

In order to surmount these constraints and to avert reproducing the same errors, Algerian firms have opted for an alternative package, the 'product-in-hand' contract. Here, long-term objectives are being reinforced to guarantee the success of technology transfer. This costly form of contract represented a panacea for avoiding the difficulties generated by turnkey contracts and hence ensuring an effective use of all installed plants as rapidly as possible. The 'product-in-hand' contract was also expected to facilitate an increase in the level of local technological capability through the hiring of foreign experts, to train local people and to facilitate learning.

2.2. Product-in-hand Contract or Plant in Production

The philosophy underlying the giving of the whole project responsibility to the technology provider, as in the 'product-in-hand' contract is to make the foreign partner feel committed to the long-term impact of the investment in terms of economical and technical achievement, the same as he/she would feel for a direct investment.

The choice for such an integrated and expensive contract is essentially motivated by the need to speed up the learning mechanisms so that local firms could use the imported technology efficiently. The contract is, therefore, aimed at procuring labour

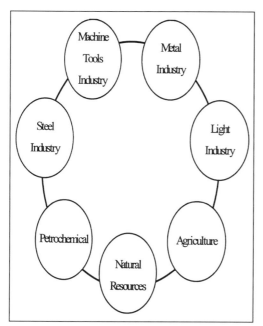

Figure 3.1: Integration of the national economy as defined by the model of industrialising industries

force training as well as enabling the production system to operate at desired rates of output and to the specified product quality levels. This integrated package has one technology supplier who is in charge of the whole project process, not only of the design, construction and commissioning of facilities but also the provisioning of the necessary skills, organisation structures and training inputs. This type of contract also aims at building up national and technological capability. It builds on the services provided by the turnkey contract, by training management and workers and by providing management and organisational assistance until the plant is run at a satisfactory level, and to international standards.

This approach allows Algerian state-owned organisations to achieve their goals regarding not only technology acquisition but also assimilation, adaptation and improvement. The supplier, as shown in Figure 3.3, is required by contract to undertake the project concept stage and to adapt it to local requirements, to train people, to be in charge of the initial management and finally to offer guarantees related to mechanical aspects, installation and performance. S/he is also required to provide technical assistance towards integrating local components as well as in manufacturing and management.

Unlike the first type of contract, the complexity of the whole technology transfer process under this contract system takes into account the need to train personnel and to give managerial assistance as well as handing over the initial management (or responsibility) for the first post-implementation stage to the technology supplier. The compatibility, or fit, between the environment and the new technology is also considered since in addition to training and to initial management, the supplier is asked to adapt the concept to local requirements and to dispense technical assistance in order to integrate local components.

Plan	1967-69	1970-73	1974-77	1980-84
Percentage of national investment allocated to industry	43 %	43%	61%	39%

Table 3.2: Percentage of investment allocated to industrialisation

	Turnkey contracts	Product-in-hand contracts
1970/73	21	1
1974/78	31	16

Table 3.3: Types and number of integrated contracts adopted between 1970 and 1978
Source: Benachenhou (1980).

Types of contracts	Purchase of machinery			Turnkey			Product-in hand		
Industries	1967/ 69	1970/ 73	1974/ 78	1967/ 69	1970/ 73	1974/ 78	1967/ 69	1970/ 73	1974/ 78
Petrochemical				3	5	8			
Iron & steel	9	3	17	0	1	1	0	0	1
Mechanical	0	0	0	1	3	3	0	1	2
Electronics	0	0	0	0	2	1	0	0	4

Table 3.4: Types of and number of contract adopted by each industry
Source: Industries et travaux d'Outre-Mer, February 1976.

Operational training is now not neglected. However, the entire responsibility for the highly integrated 'product-in-hand' project does rest with the technology supplier who carries out nearly every activity associated with the transfer. Consequently it fails to give local managers hands-on experience of project design and implementation. Cooper and Maxwell (1975) explain that such contracts can have serious negative impacts on local involvement opportunities. In the extreme, when every activity is completed wholly abroad, local managers are not given any opportunity to participate in the transfer project decision. Local managers who were not fully involved in key activities such as choice, feasibility studies, installation and project management were often lacking motivation and missing important learning opportunities (Said Amer, 1978; Perrin, 1983). This lack of involvement of end users and local managers is considered to be one of the main inhibitors to successful innovation and implementation (Leonard-Barton and Deschamps, 1988; Shaw, 1996; Tidd *et al.*, 1997). This view is also supported by Gruenfeld and Foltman (1967) who argue that the diffusion of innovation is significantly related to the involvement and motivation of end users. For Cooper (1980) and Yachir (1983), this type of contract is unlikely to promote innovation in developing countries.

By allocating greater responsibility to the technology supplier, this type of project has been successful in significantly reducing delays for project completion. However, what may have been saved in terms of time has been lost in terms of learning to operate, adapt and manage innovation.

Another important weakness of this type of contract follows the ardent desire of the technology provider to reduce risk as much as possible and, hence, to deal with well-known foreign subcontractors rather than less experienced local firms. Hoffman and Girvan (1990) report that 'foreign consultants responsible for preparing feasibility studies often recommend a package of foreign techniques and suppliers'. The economic

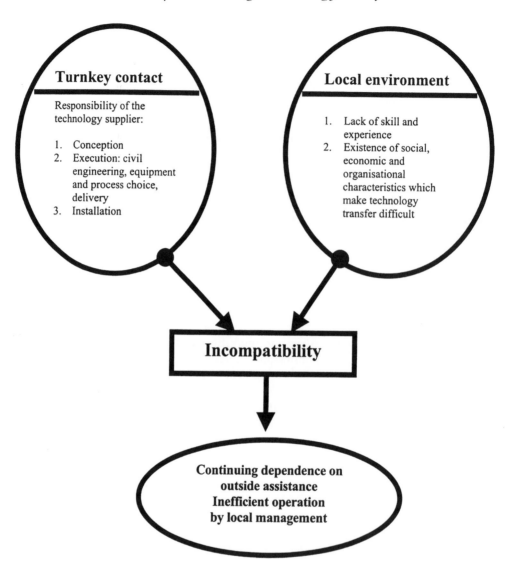

Figure 3.2: Main characteristics of a turnkey contract and its impact on the Algerian environment

integration and rapid industrialisation targeted by the Algerian policy is, therefore, not achieved as initially anticipated by the Central Plan.

2.3. The Impact of Integrated Contracts

From 1967 to 1978, US$70 billion were invested in industrialisation, but the additional production obtained did not exceed US$1.5 billion. The ratio Investment-Added Value was just about 6 to 1. The production capacity utilisation was as low as 35–40%.[2] The existing body of literature on the analysis of Algerian industrial development is quite unanimous as to the failure of this experience. The analysts are, however, divided on the reasons for this negative assessment.

One line held by Hveen (1978), Benachenhou (1980), Boutaleb (1980), Perrin (1983) and Yachir (1983), is that the Algerian Central planning mechanisms have been inefficient. For example Nellis (1980) wrote that 'in an increasingly regulated, increasingly supervised and increasingly inefficient world, the Algerian bureaucracy maintains its standing as one of the most difficult with which to deal and one of the least productive in terms of output'. For these reasons Benachenhou[3] (1980) suggests reinforcing and decentralising the planning system. His ideas of a decentralised planning system have been used as basic principles of the restructuring of state firms in 1980 and which are examined in Chapter 6.

Benissad (1982), Osterkamp (1982), Bouzidi (1986) and Bouyacoub (1987) argue that the failure is mainly the result of the non-existence of a market-orientation policy and recommend the use of the market as the major economic parameter and to run state firms on a financial profitability basis. A more recent body of literature questions the role of the state and the strong interaction between the economic and political systems which have been inhibiting efficiency, initiative and competitiveness (Goumeziane, 1994; Hassan, 1996).

This non-achievement of the anticipated objectives in terms of production, as well as in terms of assimilation and understanding of the acquired technology, has given rise to the emergence of a new way of acquiring technology, whereby local skill is fully integrated in the whole process of technology transfer.

2.4. Other Types of Contract: the 'Decomposed' or 'Design and Installation Supervised' Contract

As a result of the improvement of bargaining capability through information, acquisition, diversification of partners and technical training programmes, Algerian organisations started feeling a vital need to disintegrate, or unpack, projects as much as possible to enable and encourage their participation in the whole process of technology transfer. This has, however, led to a multiplication of contracts, partners and therefore responsibilities. The user, or technology recipient, is now in charge of co-ordinating the overall activities of the process but the project is more fragmented, the higher are the number of contracts, specialities and partners; this can make coordination complex. It is worth noting that this approach has shown to be feasible in Far Eastern countries. Its success is more demanding in terms of the capability and availability of indigenous skills than are required as a result of the increased responsibilities allocated to the local work force.

The phases prior to installation, such as knowledge awareness, exploration, selection and planning, previously left to the technology supplier in the integrated contracts, are now taken charge of by Algerian users in order to reduce implementation uncertainty. The choice is currently motivated by the need to acquire a technology which is competitive, can be assimilated, is adaptable and is compatible with local requirements. For this, the supplier is required to provide Algerian firms with technical documentation, technical assistance and supervision in order to facilitate the

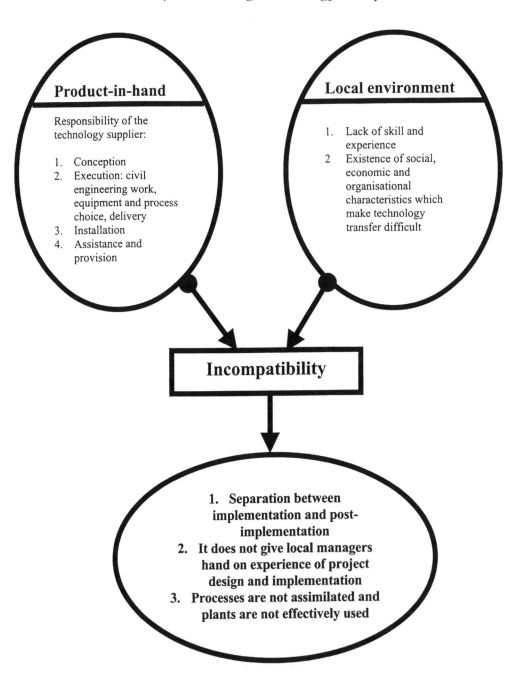

Figure 3.3: Main characteristics of Product-in-hand contact and its impact on the Algerian environment

understanding and the acquisition of knowledge by local firms and hence improve their technological capability.

This form of contract is, therefore, designed to improve the process of learning for the local organisations while projects are correctly and efficiently implemented under the supervision of the technology suppliers. It is a less costly approach since the completion is carried out by local people. Dahmani (1985), for instance, argues that in Algeria the cost of a foreign engineer is as high as five to ten times the cost of a local engineer. It is, however, important to bear in mind that such an approach, although it develops indigenous capability, leads systematically to a diversification of suppliers, processes, machineries and systems which will make assimilation, organisation, maintenance, integration and management quite complex to handle.

In this type of contract, and unlike the integrated package, the advantage expected from technology implementation is not the only factor taken into account when making a choice. Complexity and compatibility must be equally considered. This strategy also puts weight on personnel training so that assimilation, adaptation and improvement of technology can be efficiently gained. This 'decomposed' contract appears to be in line with the theory advocated by Bell (1982, 1984) and others that organisations from developing countries cannot mature unless they accumulate the capability for technological change through learning processes. As a consequence of this learning, the decomposed contract should allow savings from bargaining with various technology suppliers, together with the inclusion of local components and materials, all under the control of local management. Indeed the managing director of the Algerian Enterprise for Electricity and Gas (SONELGAZ)[4] suggests that this form of contract equips Algerian organisations with the ability to be flexible and to deal efficiently with changes. Hoffman and Girvan (1990) also support the concept that unpacking is very attractive for firms from developing countries as it can result in financial savings and above all, in increased local learning opportunities.

The construction of a local stock of technological capability has, at last, begun to be established. The quantitative and qualitative level of manpower, both scientific and technical, required by organisations to effectively use the imported technology is being strategically built.

2.5. The Algerian Scientific and Technical Context

In parallel with the installation of new plants, the development of a scientific and technical framework has also been given fundamental priority. The aim was to create the necessary conditions which would lead to the adaptation and renewal of technology. The main objective was to enable firms to use technology successfully and create compatibility between it and both the local short- and long-term needs. This was to be carried out through two major approaches.

i.   The first, mainly concerned with the long-term actions such as education, training and promotion of research activities, was taken charge of by the government. Their purpose was two-fold, first, to supply the country with a higher level of scientific and technical knowledge and, secondly, to develop the research institutions towards launching the R&D activities within the country.

ii.   The second approach was to encourage organisations to take on the tasks of acquisition and assimilation of the new technology and hence to operate new production facilities efficiently.

The double objective of this strategy can be formulated as follows:
*   to equip firms in the short term, with the necessary skills to successfully adopt and use innovation in the production sphere through an efficient operation of the newly installed plants;
*   to establish at a macro-level and in the long term, conditions which will sustain and generate innovation.

Dahmani (1985) explains the Algerian strategy as constructing a substantial stock of technological capability, based on the following conceptual models.

3. Conceptual Models Used by Algeria to Build Up Local Technological Capability

3.1. The 'Top Down' Approach
The objective of this model is to establish a local scientific and technological knowledge base which will promote innovation and develop the necessary R&D activities. It is a model which depends on central government taking long-term actions and it involves high economic risks. State-owned companies in Algeria do not feel committed to this model since the research institutions are initiated by central government and are accountable to the ministry concerned for their specific activities.

3.2. The 'Follower Model': an Approach from the Centre
This model is used by organisations which are not in a position to undertake R&D and hence to introduce major or radical innovation. The strategy is to wait for changes to appear in the market and then adopt as quickly as possible. This however, does require R&D to initiate minor or incremental innovation, for example, adaptations to local conditions and requirements. It also requires high flexibility and responsiveness. This approach is presented as not time and cost consuming but as requiring a substantial level of technological capacity, i.e. awareness and understanding skills.

3.3. The 'Bottom Up' Approach
This model is targeted at creating a local scientific and technological infrastructure, that is developing local skills to take charge of the activities such as design, implementation, operation, and management, and integration of local components. It is a global strategy model which requires time, cost and manpower. Dahmani argues that this approach requires three to four times the number of engineers needed as is by the approach from the centre. In this model, innovation is of an incremental type and arises as a means to find solutions to manufacturing problems such as quality, scrap, organisation of work, waiting time, utilisation of machines and maintenance.

3.4. Approach by Speciality or by Sector

In this approach the sectors are identified in relation to their importance to the national economy (e.g. electronics, computing, telecommunications). It is a horizontal approach since it addresses different areas of the industry and, hence, requires a wider range of knowledge. In terms of innovation, this approach generates major changes since its aim is to develop a whole and an entirely new industry in a developing country.

3.5. Combined Approach

This model combines some of above approaches aiming to avert their disadvantages. The success of this model is highly dependent on the availability of a substantial stock of indigenous skill which must be aware of the key features of the diverse approaches and capable of making 'intelligent choices'.

As a consequence of a situation where R&D infrastructure is not available and where industries such as electronics, computing, nuclear and telecommunications are given priority in investment, the Algerian strategy is, in fact, a combination of the speciality and centre approaches.

However, the ambitious aim of the Algerian policy to catch up as rapidly as possible with the development of science and technology, provides grounds to suggest that the Algerian strategy is a combination of more than these two models. The desire to obtain new manufacturing plants through the use of advanced technology, which will be rapidly operational to international qualitative and quantitative standards, is the reason for massive education, qualitative training, development of electronics, computing, design, development activities and other vital specialities. Thus, in addition to the models exposed by Dahmani, the Algerian strategy seems to include elements advocated by the top model such as the institution of Research Centres, whose objectives are to promote and generate innovation in the long term. These research institutions are essentially concerned with major, or radical, innovation. These require heavy cost and extended time for development, which firms are not generally in a position to afford. The use of 'product-in-hand' and 'decomposed' contracts also suggest that principles of the bottom-up approach are incorporated in the Algerian strategy. Both types of contract are, in fact, used to develop local skills to take charge of the whole process of manufacturing and to enable local firms to adapt and improve the imported technology. Organisations are being asked to carry out minor or incremental innovation in order to gain the best of the technology transferred and to enhance their performance.

Overall it appears that local firms are being marginalised, *vis-à-vis* long-term research activities This seems to be creating a lack of coordination between the long-term and short-term programmes of innovation. Long-term research objectives, as put forward by a senior manager of one of the companies examined, are defined by bureaucrats regardless of markets and organisational requirements.

Four major criticisms can be levelled at the Algerian pattern of technology transfer based on complex and highly integrated packages:

i.   The debate regarding the Algerian development policies at a micro-level is almost non-existent. This is substantiated by the Algerian industrialisation policy (industrialising industries) which gave much more importance to a macroeconomic analysis. The organisation and its development have been placed in a secondary position by the Central Plan. The objectives regarding investments, job creation and production are set by the Government. The micro-economic focus has also been hindered by the difficulty in gaining access to companies, the lack of a research tradition and the confidentiality requirements. This book attempts to fill this gap by focusing on two in-depth case studies.

ii.   The approach so far adopted by Algeria does not involve local managers at the implementation phase, defined by Voss (1985) as the 'user process which encompasses the action from the purchase and the installation through to the successful use of technology'. As a consequence, local skills are not developed by the projects at installation. Rodrigues (1985) goes further and strongly recommends that 'if managers in developing countries want to be more involved in their country's development, they must possess a greater understanding of how to implement technology'.

iii.   Technology transfer arrangements often suffer from the weakness that too much attention is given to the hardware and too little to the software aspects of disseminating improved technologies.

iv.   It is evident that this has been carried out in a narrowly focused way developing only the minimum level of skills necessary to operate the imported technology.

The four above points confirm the description of developing countries as suggested by Stewart and James (1982) and which is characterised by:

i.   a restricted availability of technical knowledge and information;

ii.   a vast number of social, organisational and economic features, which can make it difficult or impossible to replicate off-the-shelf technology previously developed and used in developed countries.

This confirms that different selection environment and different technology trajectories occur in developing countries. Thus, technology cannot be just an item to be bought, nor a piece of hardware to be transported from one place to another, as believed in developing countries such as Algeria during the 1970s oil boom. The success of transfer of technology is the emergence of a domestic technological capacity.

Notes

1   With the shift to market economy, Algeria is currently trying hard to develop its economy and acquire new technology through FDI.

2   Results of the decade 1968–1978, published by the Ministry of Planning (Bilan de la Décennie 1968-1978, Ministère de la Planification et de l'Aménagement du Territoire, Alger).

3   Professor Benachenhou is now the Minister in charge of Finances and Economy. He is working closely with the new President of Algeria, Abdelaziz Bouteflika, elected in April 1999, and whose objective is to restructure and privatise the Algerian economy.

4   Interview published by an Algerian weekly paper (Algérie Actualités) December 1989.

Chapter 4
Case Study 1: The National Enterprise of Electronics Industry (NEEI)

This state-owned organisation has the monopoly in the electronics sector and is charged with the following activities:
i. research and development;
ii. production;
iii. maintenance;
iv. import and distribution of equipment and components related to electronic appliances and medical electronics, computing and professional electronics.

It produces: black-and-white and colour TV sets, audio products (radios, car radios, radio-cassettes, cassette players and music centres), TV aerials and a wide range of electronic and non-electronic components to be integrated into the assembly of video and audio products (integrated circuits, transistors, diodes, cathode tubes, ceramic condensers, plastic condensers, electrolytic condensers, carbon resistors, wound resistors, potentiometers, speakers, transformers, coils, TV cabinets).

1. NEEI's Strategy
The development of the electronics industry in developing countries can be classified under three major headings.
i. Those countries which have no electronics industry at all.
ii. A large number of developing countries where the electronics industry is implemented through FDI. In this case, the electronics industry is essentially limited to assembly activities.
iii. Countries such as South Korea, Brazil and India, which have successfully attempted to develop an electronics industry as a national, independent and export-oriented industry. In this group, activities consist of electronic-component manufacturing rather than just assembly activities.

NEEI's approach to industrial development of electronics as defined by the Central Plan has been driven by the need to pertain to the third group and to reject importing technology via FDI. The Algerian firm's strategy is based upon the belief that assimilation of assembly techniques needs to be associated with assimilation of machinery used in the whole process of the assembly line as well as that of the whole manufacturing process of components. This explains the acquisition of integrated and complex systems of technology through highly packaged contracts and hence the construction of a large plant characterised by an important vertical integration.

1.1. Vertical Integration and its Impact on the Configuration of the Electronics Plant

The whole process of production, starting from the manufacturing of components, to the assembly of end-products is conducted in this plant. In 1989, this plant represented 92% of the firm's turnover and 65% of the total workforce[1]. It was initially constructed to produce TV sets (colour and black and white), radios, radio-cassettes, music centres, car-radios, indoor and outdoor TV aerials as well as a wide range of electronic and non-electronic components to be integrated in the assembly of end-products. Such an approach meant the use and the assimilation of:

   i.   raw materials and sub-groups to be integrated into this industry;
   ii.   electronic components;
   iii. design and development of new products;
   iv.   assembly process and testing of end-products.

The different aspects of the electronics industry initially implemented in this plant are presented in Tables 4.1–4.4.

Industry	Raw material	Techniques
1. Metallurgy	Steel, aluminium, nickel, zinc, silver, silicum, tin etc	
2. Metallic & mechanic industry	Stamped pieces, machined pieces, treated sheet-iron	Stamped, machining and steel plate manufacturing
3. Chemistry & Petrochemistry	Plastic granules and resins	Electrolysis and Chemical treatments spraying
4. Plastic	Video and audio cabinets chassis frames	Moulding
5. Electricity	Wires, cables, electrical insulating, electrical engines and micro engines, transformers	
6. Wood	Cabinets and chassis frames	

Table 4.1: Raw materials used in the electronics plant

1. Integrated circuits	7. Electrolytic condensers
2. Transistors	8. Resisters with carbon
3. Diodes	9. Wound resisters
4. Cathode ray tubes	10. Potentiometers
5. Ceramic condensers	11. Speakers
6. Plastic Condensers	12. Transformers
	13. Coils

Table 4.2: Electronic components manufactured in the electronics plant

Tests	Operations
1. Mechanical test	Checking if all components and short circuits fitted
2. Electrical test	Static and dynamic checking of circuits and components
3. Electrical- alignment	Checking all electrical parameters of sub-groups components
4. Final test of end-product	Checking of resistance to vibration and, shock, climatic tests, test of enduring and test of performance of the product.

Table 4.3: Components and end-products

Workshops	Components	1988	1989	1990	1991
Semi-conductors	Integrated circuits	4000	8000	12000	20000
	Transistors	10000	30000	48000	60000
Condensers	Polyester	10000	25000	40000	50000
	Electrolytic	10000	30000	50000	80000
	Ceramic	30000	45000	50000	60000
Resistance and potentiometers	With carbon	35000	50000	60000	70000
	Wound	2000	3000	3500	4000
	Potentiometers	4000	8000	12000	15000
Metallo-plastic Pieces*		70500	104450	11280	141000
Cathode ray Tubes	Colour TV 51 cm	-	-	20	400
	Colour			10	200
	B&W TV 44cm	100	110	11	120
	B&W TV 31 cm	150	160	16	180

Table 4.4: Production capacity of components manufacturing in thousands of units

* There are eight different metallo-plastic pieces.

The electronics plant has been in operation since 1979 and encompasses the following:

i.   manufacturing electronics, electromechanical and metalo-plastic components;

ii.   assembling electronic kits (THT, Tuners, Speakers) and finished products (TV sets and electronic kits).

This plant was originally set up to produce what is currently produced by the whole firm (video and audio products and their necessary components) and for this reason , it was designed to run 20 different workshops. In each workshop, several different technologies are still used. The manufacturing and assembly activities currently require the use of 5,000 different machines and tools, 30,000 different parts and about 1,000 sub-groups of components. Most of this plant's supplies (92%) come from abroad and as a consequence, NEEI deals with 2,000 different suppliers.

This plant was initially divided into the following six departments because of the large number of techniques and technologies used:

i.   Assembly department with two major assembly lines:

       a   finished products (video, audio, aerials and tuners);

       b   sub-assembly operations of components (coils, printed circuits, monitoring commands).

ii.   Department of semi-conductors.

iii.   Department of active components manufacturing with six workshops:

       a.   THT for black and white TV sets;

       b.   THT for colour TV sets;

       c.   deflectors for black and white TV sets;

       d.   coils;

       e.   speakers;

       f.   transformers and other electronic components.

iv.   Department of cathode ray tubes.

v.   Department of passive manufacturing components with six different workshops:

       a.   resistors with carbon;

       b.   wound resistances;

       c.   electrolytic condensers;

       d.   ceramic condensers;

       e.   polyester condensers;

       f.   potentiometers.

vi.   Department with various workshops:

       a.   stamping;

       b.   plastic mouldings;

       c.   wood cabinets;

       d.   surface-treatments;

       e.   printed circuits;

       f.   aerials.

Tables 4.1–4.4 show the complex dimension of this plant. As a result of this complexity and the shortage of in-house skills, assimilation was low. As a consequence, the foreign technology supplier and constructor of this plant was requested to run the department of materials and supplies for two years (1978/79) as a part of the packaged contract.

The variety of products, activities and supplies has made the management and co-ordination between the different departments and workshops extremely arduous for the inexperienced Algerian workforce. As a consequence, it has been difficult to manufacture products on schedule, meeting both satisfactory quality and cost criteria. The complex interactions between the different departments and workshops have made it impossible to optimise use of production capacity as shown in Tables 4.5 and 4.6.

To surmount these difficulties and improve its management as well as the understanding of assembly and components manufacturing, NEEI decided to reduce the complexity of the electronics plant and to focus on the manufacturing of the following components:

i.   cathode-tubes;
ii.   semi-conductors;
iii.   condensers;
iv.   resistors and potentiometers;
v.   metallic and plastic components;
vi.   printed circuits.

This action is named by the firm as the 'redeployment' of the electronics plant.

1.2. The Redeployment and Its Objectives

The first objective of this redeployment was to increase the production capacity of the whole firm by transferring the simple assembly activities to two new plants. The second objective was to reorganise the electronics plant in order to reduce its complexity and enable it to concentrate on core activities.

One aerial plant with 230 employees and one audio plant with 220 employees were set up as a result of transfer from the electronics plant of the TV aerial assembly line in 1985 and the audio- assembly line in 1986. The audio-plant produces radios, radio cassettes, cassette players, and music centres and has a workforce of 220.

Before transfer						After transfer				
1979	1980	1981	1982	1983	1984	1985	1986	1987	1988	1989
150	180	280	280	280	280	280	450	700	700	700

Table 4.5: The production capacity of TV aerials (in thousands of units)

Before transfer						After transfer				
1979	1980	1981	1982	1983	1984	1985	1986	1987	1988	1989
510	510	375	305	355	355	370	600	600	600	700

Table 4.6:The production capacity of audio products (in thousands of units)

Both the audio and aerial plants were constructed by NEEI itself as a consequence of the transfer of simple assembly activities from the electronics plant. Their electronic components such as coils, speakers, printed circuits, and mechanical and plastic pieces are still being manufactured by the electronics plant. Both plants were constructed by the engineering and construction department of NEEI under the supervision of the technology supplier. The company's engineering and construction department was responsible for the civil engineering work, the choice of the technology, the definition of specifications and the installation of machines. Training in the use of the additional and new equipment was provided at NEEI's training centre under the supervision of the technology supplier.

The shift of simple assembly activities to two new plants was also aimed at enabling the electronics plant with its 2,500 employees to concentrate its activities simply on the fabrication of electronic components. As a result, the electronics plant was restructured in five autonomous units:

i.   semi-conductor;
ii.   condensers;
iii.   resistors and potentiometers;
iv.   cathode ray tubes;
v.   metallic pieces.

The area used for manufacturing components was increased from 18,000 m^2 in 1987 to 66,000 m^2 in 1990. The increase, which is as much as four-fold, is substantial. The forecast increase in production capacity was also quite ambitious but has not been attained. A serious level of recurring breakdowns and a significant level of under-utilisation of production capacity generated by a low level of understanding of imported technology has, once again, rendered the organisation unable to achieve its forecast. Another major reason is also related to the drastic reduction of imports after 1989 linked to the decline in income from oil exports and the undergoing economic crisis. The impact was even more dramatic for the electronics industry because of its high sensitivity towards external constraints resulting in its strong external dependency in terms of inputs, components and machinery.

The average increase in production capacity for all activities of manufacturing components is 230% (see Tables 4.7 and 4.8). This is less than the increase of the areas (267%) to be utilised for the manufacturing of these components. This indicates that priority is still given to acquisition of hardware. The rise in the domain of assembly activities follows a different pattern from the one put forward for the activities of components manufacturing. The increase in assembly activities is shown in Tables 4.5, 4.6, 4.9 and 4.10.

These tables show a 97% average increase in the production capacities for the assembly lines, carried out with a 29% reduction of the total assembly areas. There are three major reasons for this achievement:

i   use of machinery requiring less raw material consumption and less time for adjustment;
ii   optimisation of existing areas of assembly activities;
iii   improvement in learning.

Workshops	Components	1988	1989	1990	1991
Semi-conductors	Integrated circuits	4,000	8,000	12000	20000
	transistors	10,000	30,000	48000	60000
Condensers	Polyester	10,000	25,000	40000	50000
	Electrolytic	10,000	30,000	50000	80000
	Ceramic	30,000	45,000	50000	60000
Resistance and potentiometers	With carbon	35,000	50,000	60000	70000
	Wound	2,000	3,000	3500	4000
	Potentiometers	4,000	8000	12000	15000
Metallo-plastic Pieces*		70,500	104450	11280	141000
Cathode ray Tubes	Colour TV (51 cm)	-	-	20	400
	Colour			10	200
	Black& white TV (44cm)	100	110	11	120
	Black&white TV (31 cm)	150	160	16	180

Table 4.7: The production capacity for component manufacture (in thousands of units)

Workshops	Before redeployment(m)	After redeployment(m)	Increase(%)
Semiconductors	14	80	471
Condensers	50	190	280
Resistances and potentiometers	41	89	117
Metallo-plastic pieces	71	141	103
Cathode tubes for colour TV	No production	400,000	New manufacturing line
Black and white TV	250,000	300,000	20
Average	250,000	700,000	180

Table 4.8: The increase in capacity for component manufacture

* There are eight different metallo-plastic pieces.

Products	1980	1984	1985	1986	1987	1988
Black and White TV	100	250	405	420	420	420
Colour TV	26	90	140	140	180	315
Audio	300	370	580	600	700	700
Antennas	150	280	450	700	700	700

Table 4.9: The production capacity of finished products (Assembly capacities in thousands of units).

This suggests that there is greater use of automatic and semi-automatic machinery in the assembly lines as well as a better understanding and use of the assembly techniques. However, the pattern for the manufacturing of components is different and does suggest a low assimilation of these manufacturing techniques. This, as explained by NEEI's workers and managers, is the outcome of a series of factors including:

i   complexity of technologies used;
ii   integrated nature of the contract used, which led to the non-involvement of local management;
iii   poor availability of documentation regarding the utilisation and maintenance of machines, specifications of products, components and materials, nomenclature of products and specifications of tests.

To these notable points must be added the incompatibility between the strategy adopted to develop electronics in Algeria and the low availability, within the firm being studied and throughout the country, of in-house skill and industrial experience. The large scale of the plant and the variety of techniques and activities within this plant has made this incompatibility more significant.

The redeployment of the electronics plant was aimed at overcoming this incompatibility, increasing the production capacities and improving the assimilation of the technology used. The approach adopted for this restructuring placed a greater emphasis on the involvement of local managers throughout the whole project under the supervision of the technology supplier. More importance was also attached to the acquisition of the hardware as well as the software component of technology. As shown in Table 4.11, substantial investments have been made available for the effective transfer of information and knowledge about the purchased technology.

Products	Before redeployment	After redeployment	Increase
Black & White TV	250000	420000	68%
Colour TV	180000	315000	75%
Audio	370000	700000	88%
Antennas	280000	700000	150%

Table 4.10: Increase in assembly production

For each dinar (DA) spent on the acquisition of machinery, DA0.66 is spent on the acquisition of knowledge and information regarding this machinery. In reality, this rate comes to a higher figure as a consequence of a high recruitment of graduates and skilled workers, as shown in Table 4.12.

There is a clear tendency to recruit more graduates in the science-oriented activity of component manufacturing, in which changes are frequent and rapid. This new approach, based upon capital knowledge, is motivated by the necessary requirements associated with new technology in terms of high skill. It is aimed at avoiding errors such as those made in the past with respect to the nature of the contract and the choice of products and techniques adopted, and their impact on the firm's performance and organisation.

2. NEEI's Strategy for Technology Transfer

2.1. The Choice

The complexity and the large dimension of the electronics plant has led to a construction schedule of construction spread over six years as shown in Table 4.13.

The whole plant became fully operational in 1982. The contract with the United States partner was signed in 1974 after lengthy negotiations. This means that most of the techniques and technology used in this plant correspond to those available in the market at that period and which were therefore developed and launched in the late 1960s and early 1970s. This has led inevitably and fairly rapidly to a significant degree of obsolescence of most transferred technologies.

Cost 1: cost of machinery; *Cost 2*: cost for knowledge acquisition; *Ratio*: ratio knowledge/machinery.

Workshop	Cost 1	Licence & know-how	Foreign assistance	Training	Costs 2	Ratio
Cathode Tubes	130	40	23	25	88	0.68
Semi-Conductor	140	50	24	30	104	0.74
Condenser	30	5	6	8	19	0.63
Registers Potentiometers	20	5	3	4	12	0.6

Table 4.11: Investment for the main redeployment projects (in millions of dinars)

61

Categories of personnel	Before redeployment	After redeployment
Unskilled workers in charge of execution	70%	65%
Skilled workers	25%	22%
Graduates	5%	13%

Table 4.12: Categories of personnel in the area of components manufacturing

Tasks	Forecast schedule				Actual schedule	
	Studies		Completion		End of Studies	End of Completion
	Start	End	Start	End		
Definition of Product Machinery and Lay-out	1/1975	1/1977	-	-	6/1979	
Material of Production	1/1975	4/1978	-	-	3/1979	
Training	1/1975	2/1978	-	-	6/1979	6/1980
Operations: Organisation	1/1975	4/1975	-	-	3/1976	12/1980
Supplies	1/1977	4/1977	-	-	3/1978	6/1979
Tasks	1/1977	6/1977	-	-	6/1978	6/1980
Production	1/1977	6/1977	4/1978	3/1980	6/1978	6/1980

Table 4.13: The electronics plant's construction schedule

2.2. Nature of Obsolescence

Obsolescence has occurred at the level of finished products as well as at the level of electronic components. As mentioned above, the audio and video goods produced by NEEI correspond to the market of the late 1960s and early 1970s. For instance, the audio products (radios, cassette players, record players) chosen at that period were merely mono-function and, as soon as the electronics plant started operating, these products were already obsolete and in fierce competition with products with combined functions. These products were also obsolete in their design. The electrical design was based on the use of discrete components, leading to the consumption of a large number of them. Some of these components have even disappeared from the international market. The mechanical design was also based on the use of several cases and disconnecters on printed circuits which implied the production of large and heavy printed circuits.

The electronics component industry is characterised by rapid change and short life-cycles. However, the manufacturing process for electronic components existing in NEEI was chosen in the early 1970s. In addition, emphasis was placed on as much acquiring the greatest amount possible of manual equipment in order to create the highest possible number of jobs. This is viewed by the company's engineers as the reason for the low quality of most of their electronic components. Four examples are presented below to illustrate the type of obsolescence reflecting the nature of difficulties encountered by firms from developing countries with low skills which are endeavouring to acquire advanced technology through highly packaged contracts.

1. The semi-conductor industry is characterised by rapid and significant technological change. There is a tendency towards more miniaturisation and integration of multiple functions within the same component leading to the replacement of many components by only one. To keep abreast with the pace of technological change, the firm being studied has decided to invest in knowledge acquisition as well as in machinery acquisition. That is why, as shown in Table 4.11, the semi-conductors project investment has the highest ratio for skill and knowledge acquisition. In Table 4.14, there is also evidence of the importance given by the semi-conductors project to the recruitment of graduates and skilled workers. Of the total workforce employed in the department 40% of semi-conductors are skilled workers and graduates. This is the highest rate within the firm under study. However, the technologies currently used in the electronics plant are limited to the production of circuits of medium integration known as medium-scale integration. The large-scale integration variety is, with the current technology system, difficult to manufacture. For instance, the electronics plant has essentially been using silicon plates of two and three chips. These types of chips are being decreasingly used in the electronics industry. They are in fact replaced by silicon plates of five and six chips which are more suited to large integration and thus, better-performing and more economical.

2. The electronics plant produces three kinds of condensers: electrolytic, ceramic and plastic. The processes used are manual and do not permit a precise monitoring of the elements used in the manufacture of this electronic component. This leads inevitably to the lowering of quality and reliability in these components. For instance, the manual handling of aluminium bands during the winding of wires often results in the deterioration of the chemical characteristics of the electrolyte.

3. The wound resisters manufactured by the electronics plant are also less used in the electronics industry because of their high dissipation, bulkiness, weight and high cost.

Project Investment or Department	Shopfloor Workers in Execution	Shopfloor Workers with Skill	Graduates	TOTAL
Cathode-Tubes	400 or 67%	120 or 20%	80 or 13%	600
Semi-Conductors	300 or 60%	120 or 24%	80 or 16%	500
Condensers	300 or 75%	60 or 15%	40 or 10%	400
Resistances and Potentiometers	260 or 72%	60 or 17%	40 or 11%	360
Assembly	460 or 77%	80 or 13%	60 or 10%	600

Table 4.14: Category of workforce per project investment

4.   The potentiometers are assembled entirely manually. This has a large impact on the quality of this component. The reject rate (35%) is in fact high in this department.

An additional example of obsolescence concerns the structural organisation of the electronics plant, which is discussed in the assessment of the firm's performance.

3. Performance of NEEI

As a result of its large scale, the electronics plant, initially designed for 4,000 employees, 280 different workstations and seven hierarchical levels, has proved extremely difficult to manage. The current organisational system of the electronics plant, is based on Fordist principles with a high level of hierarchies and a strong division between departments and activities that make co-ordination and integration of the activities of the different workshops extremely difficult to tackle. The necessary interaction and exchange of information between the commercial, technical and production functions, is slow as a consequence of the organisational system currently in operation and based on a strong separation between these functions. For instance, maintenance, quality control and organisation of work fall under the responsibility of the technical department and hence are separated from the assembly and manufacturing lines, which are attached to the production department. The responsibility for supplies is allocated to the commercial department which often has no knowledge about the specificity of the supplies of each workshop. The importance of organisational change in developing countries is addressed in Chapters 6 and 8.

By examining the performance of the firm under study until 1990, it is the intention in this section to assess the organisation's strategy in acquiring and developing technological capabilities in the electronics industry. Parameters such as volumes of output, utilisation of production capacities, manpower, investments and others are used to measure and evaluate the firm's performance. The impact on the learning curves of both firms under study in this research is examined in Chapter 7.

3.1. Evolution of Volumes Output

There is a rise, except for 1986 and 1987, where the drop was due to the shortage of supplies as a result of drastic reduction of imports (see Table 4.15). The average increase, with 1979 as a base year, is 227% and the average increase from one year to another is 16.89%. However, such figures taken by themselves are meaningless. The output of this firm can be better assessed if it is compared with the existing capacity and with the forecast programme of production. From such comparisons, it is possible to draw conclusions with respect to the efficient use of the imported technologies and to the learning curve.

3.2. Utilisation of Production Capacity

The company's average capacity utilisation by the end of the 1980s was no more than 60% (seeTable 4.16). After ten years of operation full utilisation of the capacity installed is not yet reached. The shortage of supplies in 1987 and 1988 is not responsible for this considerable idle capacity. This can certainly be accounted for by the following factors:

i.   the strategy adopted by NEEI whose aim was to implement, use and learn simultaneously different technologies;

ii.   the poor level of locally available skills.

3.3. Human Resources Management

It is clear that the aspect of training and availability of in-house skills have never been neglected by the firm and the Central Plan, but the approach adopted has not enabled NEEI to achieve its objectives with respect to transfer of technology and assimilation. Table 4.17 shows the interest given by the firm to recruiting more graduates and skilled workers.

There is clear evidence that this firm, like most state-owned companies in Algeria, is over-staffed. This is the result of an objective set by the central government, namely to create as many jobs as possible. However, at company level, most managers strongly believe that an effective development of the electronics industry requires automatic equipment and less manual handling. They perceive the enhancement of their firm's performance in terms of quality, accuracy, cost reduction, lead time and flexibility only through advanced technology requiring less manpower. Indeed, most of the machinery selected for the extension of the manufacturing, assembly and quality control of electronic components was based on advanced technology and information technology. However, for political reasons and when possible, a second assembly and manufacturing line was installed with semi-automatic equipment in order to keep the workforce employed. Furthermore, a large proportion of the workforce belonging to category one and in charge of the execution of production are illiterate. This is why Tables 4.12, 4.13 and 4.17 show a clear tendency towards more graduates and skilled workers. However, a substantial number of these skilled workers and even engineers have benefited from internal promotion and do not possess the required skill for the job they are carrying out.

	Black and White TV	Colour TV	Audio	Aerials
1979	54000	10000	24000	24000
1980	76000	21000	49000	49000
1981	119000	27000	144000	144000
1982	126000	48000	227000	227000
1983	152000	62000	232000	232000
1984	210000	82000	252000	252000
1985	238000	87000	194000	194000
1986	262000	120000	348000	348000
1987	224000	92000	543000	543000
1988	181000	119000	377000	377000

Table 4.15: The output for the major products of NEEI

	Black & White TV		Colour TV		Audio		Aerials	
	1	**2**	**1**	**2**	**1**	**2**	**1**	**2**
1979	100	54%	26	37%	510	3%	150	16%
1980	100	76%	26	80%	510	28%	180	27%
1981	100	119%	60	45%	375	53%	280	51%
1982	180	70%	60	80%	305	58%	280	81%
1983	210	72%	75	82%	355	63%	280	83%
1984	250	84%	90	91%	355	65%	280	90%
1985	300	79%	90	97%	370	76%	280	69%
1986	340	77%	140	86%	600	55%	450	77%
1987	405	55%	100	92%	600	32%	700	785
1988	420	43%	140	85%	660	345	700	71%
1989		73%		77%		48%		64%

Table 4.16: Production capacity and rate of utilisation of production capacity

3.4. Other Measurement Parameters

The annual turnover growth is around 33%. However, as shown in Table 4.18, the overheads are substantial. The increase in the cost of labour is higher than the increase of production. The stock of raw materials is significantly high, and corresponds to 11

	Category 3		Category 2		Category 1		Total Work Force
		%		%		%	
1980	254	4.5%	1377	24.6%	2965	71.8%	5596
1981	260	4.6%	1370	24.4%	3970	71%	5600
1982	267	4.8%	1370	24.4%	3970	70.8%	5607
1983	280	5%	1376	24.5%	3960	70.5%	5616
1984	330	5.7%	1425	24.7%	4023	69.6%	5778
1985	389	6.6%	1425	24.4%	4023	69%	5837
1986	410	7%	1440	24.4%	4040	68.6%	5890
1987	526	8.7%	1458	24%	4062	67.3%	6046
1988	607	10%	1440	23.6%	4044	66.4%	6091
1989	647	10.3%	1500	24%	4124	65.7%	6271

Category 3: Graduates and engineers
Category 2: Shopfloor workers with speciality (skilled workers)
Category 1: Shopfloor workers without skill in charge of the execution

Table 4.17: Workforce in NEEI by category of personnel

months of annual consumption. In 1985, NEEI started making profits, but, in 1987 and in 1988, the result was negative.[5]

The presentation of NEEI's strategy and performance cannot be considered as a positive achievement. The above figures show a clear and positive evolution of the production volume, but full use of capacity has not yet been achieved since the current rate of use is not higher than 60%. The increase in the total overheads is significantly higher than the increase of the output volume. The firm is overstaffed as a result of the decision imposed by the central government to create as many jobs as possible. It is under-qualified and has a limited experience in this industry characterised by rapid technological changes.

The strategy adopted by NEEI was aimed at developing an electronics industry as a national, independent and export-oriented activity. The assimilation of assembly techniques was to be linked with the assimilation of machinery used in the whole process of the assembly line (insertion, welding, testing) as well as the assimilation of components manufacturing. This ambitious choice has led to the construction of plants in which the entire process of production, starting from the manufacturing of components, to the assembly of end-products is completed. This strategy based, on vertical integration, means the assimilation of various techniques regarding:

i.   the raw materials and sub-groups integrated as inputs in the manufacturing process;
ii.   the electronic components;
iii.   the design and development of new products;
iv.   the assembly process and test of end-products.

However, the success of such a strategy is strongly linked to the availability of a substantial level of local capability which in the case of most developing countries is lacking. The negative result identified in the above analysis is therefore accounted for by the incompatibility between:

	1983	1984	1985	1986	1987	1988
Turnover	760	1026	1385	1684	1660	2656
Production	778	1111	1531	1542	1356	1364
Personnel Overheads	170	190	210	274	274	280
Raw Materials Consumption	320	390	440	442	464	479
Raw Materials Stock	290	360	360	353	456	481
Gross Financial Result	-160	-117	20	106	-48	-22

Table 4.18: Major parameters from 1983 to 1988

i.   the complex strategy adopted by the firm;
ii.   the lack of in-house skills.

Both factors, as discussed in Chapters 1, 2 and 3 inhibit technology transfer, diffusion and learning.

In order to improve the assimilation of the technology used and to increase its performance, NEEI has endeavoured to re-organise its manufacturing plants. The aim is to separate the manufacturing activities as well as to place emphasis on activities such as electronic components manufacturing. However, more importance is still being given to the acquisition of the physical aspect of technology (hardware) with a greater emphasis placed on the acquisition of more automatic and semi-automatic machinery. Hence, the difficulty to tackle the incompatibility between the complexity of the imported technology, and the low-level local capabilities.

Notes

1   The Electronics Enterprise (NEEI) has over 5,000 employees and five different plants (electronics plant, TV plant, TV aerial plant, audio plant and medical equipment plant)
2   The Algerian currency (dinar: DA) has since been drastically devalued. See Figure 4.1.
3   After 1989, the shortage of supplies occurred more frequently as a result of a drastic fall of imports.
4   The level of capacity utilisation has also been in decline since 1989, and throughout the 1990s as a result of the current and lasting economic crisis.
5   The results remain negative throughout the 1990s and like most state-owned companies, NEEI is currently being restructured in order to be privatised.

1987	$1= DA 4.9
1988	$1= DA 6.7
1990	$1= DA 12
1992	$1= DA 22.8
1994	$1= DA 35.1
1996	$1= DA 56.2
1998	$1= DA 61

Figure 4.1.

Chapter 5
Case Study 2: The National Enterprise of Farm Machinery (NEFM)

NEFM with 7,232 employees, was allocated the monopoly of the farm machinery industry and therefore given charge of the following activities: R&D, production, distribution, maintenance, and import and export of agricultural equipment and machinery. Its production range is diversified and includes:

i.   three types of tractors;
ii.   four types of engines (tractors, lorries, combine-harvester and mechanical appliance);
iii.   agricultural vehicles transport (trucks and trailers);
iv.   farm machinery ploughs, disc-ploughs;
v.   sowing machinery;
vi.   fertilisation machinery;
vii   agricultural treatment machinery;
viii.   parts.

NEFM's plants can be divided into two major groups. The first group consists of two large plants, which were constructed in the 1970s through the use of highly packaged forms of contracts. The second group comprises three small-to-medium plants which utilise simple technology. Local managers were greatly involved in the construction of the second group of plants and in the choice and installation of their technology.

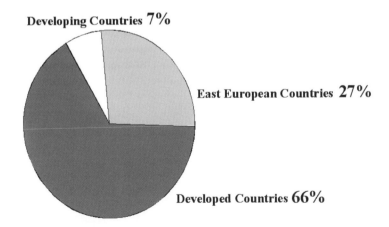

Figure 5.1: Distribution of farm machinery equipment

1. NEFM's Strategy for Technology Transfer

Figure 5.1 shows how the world production of farm machinery equipment is distributed.

The pace of technological change and the heavy investment it requires, has led to an important concentration within this industry as a result of mergers and take-overs. The technology of agricultural machinery and equipment is undergoing considerable change as a consequence of the increasing introduction of micro-electronics, automation and information technology, which manifests itself in the proliferation of computer-aided machine tools and robots for various applications such as welding, spraying and assembling. This explains the very slight participation (7% of the world production) of firms from developing countries in this industry. The involvement of developing countries in this highly competitive industry can be summarised as fitting to one of the three following groups.

i. A group which carries out merely assembly activities.
ii A group with manufacturing capacities and in which 20–30% of local components are integrated in their production.
iii A group with manufacturing capacities in which more than 50% of local components are integrated in their production. South Korea, Mexico, Argentina, India, Brazil, Yugoslavia and China are included in this group.

The Algerian state-owned company was requested by the Central Plan to work towards joining the third group in order to help the country to develop a high level of farm machinery production with a view to satisfying local needs and exporting. This justifies the purchase of expensive, integrated and complex systems of technology through a highly packaged contract – product-in-hand. It also explains the wide diversity of activities available in the two major plants of the firm.

Three separate phases can be identified in the strategy adopted to acquire and expand the mechanical and farm equipment industry in Algeria.

i. A high measure of investment to implement this industry in Algeria through construction of large plants with a high level of integration.
ii. Rationalisation of the capacities installed in phase one.
iii. Renewal of production capacities in order to update and upgrade the technology used and sustain international competitiveness.

1.1. Extensive Development Phase

The first phase corresponds to the implementation of this industry during the 1970s through 'product-in-hand' contracts with the construction of the engine and tractor plant (3,446 employees) and the farm machinery plant (1,600 employees). Both plants were large and designed to manufacture a wide range of products.

The initial purpose of the engine and tractors plant was to produce ten different end-products as well as the parts required for these end-products. For this, the six following major workshops were installed within the same plant.

1. Smelting.
2. Boiler-making.

3. Machining:
    i. machining line for production means;
    ii. machining line for track links and breech blocks;
    iii. machining for small batches (grinding);
    iv. machining for large-sized parts (boring).
4. Thermal treatment.
5. Assembly:
    i. production means assembly;
    ii. engine assembly;
    iii. tractor assembly;
    iv. testing bench;
    v. production control.
6. Workshop for diverse activities:
    i. spraying;
    ii. distribution of energies and fluids;
    iii. handling materials;
    iv. transport means.

The farm machinery plant was also designed to manufacture 33 different products belonging to the four following groups:
i. farm machinery;
ii. sowing machinery;
iii. fertilisation machinery;
iv. treatment machinery and a wide range of parts to be integrated to the finished products.

As a result, this plant is operating with 300 machine tools and 10,000 to 12,000 components. The combine harvester, for instance, requires 7,000 different components, of which 2,000 are manufactured in the same plant. In comparison, to produce the same combine harvester, the German constructor and owner of the licence, uses five different plants which do not produce more than 30% of the required components. The rest is provided by a large group of external sub-contractors.

Consequently, various technologies of high density were implemented in these two plants, for which the level of qualification and experience of the workforce was simply not adequate. These firms had also to cope with a diversified number of supplies which needed to be imported from abroad. This has inevitably led to constant stoppages of production, frequent bottlenecks and under-utilisation of structural capacities (35%). This is why the second phase of NEFMs strategy was aimed at rationalising existing potential by giving to each of their manufacturing plants a specialist function and optimising their production process.

1.2. Intensive Development Phase

The objective of this phase was to reduce the complexity of the large plants by limiting their operations to core activities. The tractor plant was restructured to focus on the

	1974	1975	1976	1977	1978	1979	1980	1981	1982	1983	Forecasted production
Tractors	661	1577	1834	2839	3923	4886	4206	4379	4500	6002	5000
Engines	882	2024	3252	3481	4910	6210	7631	7051	7401	10054	9500
Combine Harvesters	NOP	NOP	NOP	NOP	116	371	415	385	416	601	500

Table 5.1: NEFM's major products from 1974–83.

production of engines and the assembly of tractors. The activities and the range of products of the farm machinery plant were reorganised and limited to combine-harvesters, hay-makers and harrows. The sowing equipment, fertilisation equipment and treatment equipment were transferred to other plants. This has led to a substantial increase in the utilisation of capacity, and production (see Table 5.1).[1]

A period of seven to ten years practice has enabled the two plants to reach the planned volume of output. As shown in Tables 5.1 and 5.2, this has been achieved gradually. However, there is still considerable idle capacity in both plants. The two examples also prove that the more highly integrated and complex the plants are in terms of both the size and the technologies used, the more difficult it is to run them efficiently. The farm machinery plant, which was constructed three years after the tractors plant, has achieved a better rate of capacity utilisation and in a shorter time. This can be interpreted as a form of organisational learning acquired from the experience of the tractors project and transferred to the farm machinery project. It can also be translated as an indication of local competence to use and manage simpler systems of technology. This is confirmed by the ability not only to achieve but also to surpass the predicted production of hay-makers, in which a simple technology has been used as far back as 1980.

In 1986, although 90% of the machinery used by NEFM's plants was of conventional type, the rate of capacity utilisation in these plants was less than 60% and the scrap rate was as high as 30%. NEFM's managers attribute this poor performance to the 14-year-old machine tools available within their plants and the difficulties of maintaining them. This, according to the managers interviewed was the main reason for production stoppages, bottlenecks, the high rate of scrap and the poor quality of products.

1.3. Acquisition of Advanced Technology

The third phase of NEFM's strategy is aimed at enabling the firm to enhance its performance by the use of new equipment based on advanced and information technology.

	1977	1978	1979	1980	1981	1982	1983	1984
Tractor Plant	36	41	43	44	46	48	50	52
Farm Machinery Plant	30	34	39	42	45	50	57	57

Table 5.2: The rate of capacity of utilisation: 1977–84

Activities	Percentage
Smelting	10%
Boilermaking	8%
Machining	17%
Assembly	50%
Technical Support	5%
Diverse Activities	10%

Table 5.3: New machinery investments in the tractors plant.

The purpose is to replace three to four conventional machine tools by new machinery and an equipement base embodying more advanced technology. In the tractors plant, for instance, a flexible cell has been selected to replace three lathes in the manufacturing of two types of engines block and two types of gear box. Computer numerical controlled (CNC) machine tools have also been installed to control grinding and boring activities within the machining workshop. Assembly activities and final test activities have also been re-inforced by the use of automatic machinery. Table 5.3 gives the distribution of new equipment investments per activity in the tractors plant and show the significant emphasis placed on automated finished lines in order to improve assembly, controlling and testing of end products.

In the farm machinery plant, a flexible cell has also been installed for the manufacture of two types of gear box (combine harvester and hay-maker) and their components. Numerical control (NC) and CNC machines are currently used in sliding, turning and grinding lathe activities as well as drilling, milling, nibbling and stamping. The use of more advanced technology is aimed at improving the quality and the life of combine harvesters. Table 5.4 gives an indication of the life of the major products of NEFM. Unlike products from industrialised countries, the short life of NEFM's products is another indication of their poor quality level.

The cost related to the acquisition of the advanced technology is not considered to be excessively high as three to four conventionally controlled machines are being replaced by one piece of advanced technology equipment. Jacobson *et al.* (1983) argue that maturation of new technology has simplified its learning and reduced substantially its price per unit.

With the use of new technology, NEFM is planning to increase its overall production by as much as 42% and raise its level of capacity utilisation from 53% to 85% in 1990. It was also anticipated that the introduction of advanced technology would improve the organisation of production processes by reducing bottlenecks and lead time. In addition to increasing the production output, productivity and reducing production cost, it was also expected that the new technology would enhance the quality level.

However, an assessment of the first experience in the acquisition of new technology machine tools by NEFM, has highlighted how difficult it was to achieve integration of

	NEFM		Europe	
	Normative	Actual	Normative	Normative
Combine Harvesters	10 years	6 years	12 years	15 years
Tractors	7 years	5 years	8 years	10 years

Table 5.4: A comparison between the life time of European and NEFM's tractors and combine harvesters.

the new machine tools within the different workshop activities. As a consequence, bottlenecks have persisted in production lines. These bottlenecks are due to the difficulty in co-ordinating and managing the processes of the fast production capacities of the new machine tools and old machines which cannot function at the same pace. This led to a slowing down in the production flow which has resulted in the stock-piling of semi-finished products. This clearly indicates the importance of a more holistic approach in the acquisition and implementation of new technology, which was simply lacking in the Algerian case. The impact of new technology on the entire process of production has not been fully investigated. As a result, maintenance, which still gives rise to production stoppages, can be interpreted as yet further evidence of incompatibility between the level of in-house skill and the new technology used.

2. Assessment of NEFM's Performance

A full analysis of the strategy adopted by NEFM is undertaken in this section, which is preoccupied with assessing the development of parameters such as volume of output, utilisation of production capacity, manpower, investment and financial parameters.

2.1. Organisation of Manufacturing Plants

The firm's performance depends essentially on the activities of the tractors and farm machinary plants in which new technology is used to manufacture the major products of the firm such as engines, tractors, combine-harvesters, hay-makers and the parts to be integrated in the manufacturing of these end-products. For these reasons, the present study focuses primarily on the performance of these two plants whose turnover represents 95% of firm's turnover and employ around 70% of the total workforce.

The poor performance of their plants has three main causes:

i.   complexity of technology used and lack of technical documentation regarding its functioning;
ii.   chronic shortage of supplies;
iii.   low qualification level of the workforce.

The first two causes can be considered as a direct consequence of the decision to acquire and develop the farm machinery industry through the construction of large plants with a diversity of technologies and a wide range of products. In spite of the rationalisation phase undertaken in the early 1980s, these plants are still inefficiently run as a consequence of the enduring incompatibility between the systems of technology imported and the national economy and its systems of innovation.

This complexity has been exacerbated by an organisation significantly marked by a strong separation of functions and a pyramidal and hierarchical type of structure that will be examined in greater details in Chapter 6.

This separation of functions is also marked at the production level which leads to a proliferation of decision-making centres whose coordination is extremely difficult to achieve. It also creates a heavy and long flow of information which inevitably implies delays in execution of tasks.

The major functions or specialised areas of these plants are also fragmented. The manufacturing function in the tractor plant is, for instance, divided into several structures depending on different decision-making centres. The splitting of this major activity leads systematically to incoherence in planning and execution of tasks and co-ordination.

The separation of complementary functions, such as production and technique or supplies and inventory, acts against integration of the production activity and thus impedes the performance of operational structures.

2.2. Human Resources Management

The major characteristics of human resources management within the organisation being studied are:

i.   lack of a sufficient number of graduates and qualified workers;
ii.   low level of industrial experience;
iii.   overstaffing.

The total number of employees has increased by 23% while, for the same period, the firm has not undertaken any new plant construction. This period was, in fact, essentially devoted to rationalisation and optimisation of existing potentialities in order to enhance the firm's performance.

The technical support workforce is the only category undergoing a significant increase while the workforce employed in production and administration is decreasing. This can be explained by the strategy adopted by NEFM, which puts emphasis on activities such as development, maintenance, work organisation, planning of production, quality control and other technical activities in order to promote innovation and ensure better support for the execution of the production function. This is why the structure of the workforce of the organisation being studied is shifting towards more graduates and skilled operatives shown in Table 5.8.

In 1987, the firm recruited a large number of graduates for its research and development department and from 1980 to 1988, the number of graduates increased by as much as three-fold.

1980	1981	1982	1983	1984	1985	1986	1987	1988
5836	5927	6275	6562	6680	6700	6736	7212	7232

Table 5.6: Workforce in NEFM

	1980	1981	1982	1983	1984	1985	1986	1987	1988
Production	46	43	43	42	42	43	42	42	41
Technical Support	29	31	30	30	30	30	32	32	33
Administration	25	26	27	28	28	27	26	26	26

Table 5.7: Distribution of workforce by percentage.

	1980	1981	1982	1983	1984	1985	1986	1987	1988
Category 1	79	81	80	80	80	79.5	79.3	77.9	77.5
Category 2	17.8	17	17.3	16.6	16.4	16.4	16.3	16.3	16.3
Category 3	2.7	2.5	2.8	2.8	3.3	3.5	4.1	4.4	5.9

Category 1: personnel in charge of the execution
Category 2: personnel having a skill or a specialisation often at a supervisory level
Category 3: executives and senior managers.

Table 5.8: Distribution of workforce by category and percentage

Types of Qualification	1983	1987
Engineers	31%	33.6%
Degrees in scientific areas	7%	15.8%
Degrees in non-scientific areas	15%	7%
Internal promotions	47%	43.6%

Table 5.9: Comparison between the different qualifications of managers (1983 and 1987).

However, a considerable number of workers classified as graduates gained their position through internal promotion and, as admitted in an internal document of the organisation, do not possess the appropriate level of qualification to perform their job efficiently. Table 5.9 shows the important proportion of internal promotions within the ranks of the graduate workers (category 3) in NEFM.

This internal promotion accounts for one of the reasons for the limited level of in-house skill and the low performance of management in NEFM.

The performance of the firm is also impeded by the low qualification and poor experience of other categories of personnel. Category 1, which represents about 80% of the whole workforce, is essentially employed in activities related to production and is underqualified. As many as 16% of these workers are illiterate. This inevitably affects the execution of production tasks and can, to some extent, be used to explain the relatively poor performance of the organisation (see Table 5.10).

The impact of the low qualification of NEFM's workforce on the effective use of the imported technology can also be evaluated by examining parameters such as the utilisation of production capacities and production volume.

Production	67%
Technical Support	13%
Administration	20%

Table 5.10: Category 1 by sector of activity(%).

	Combine-Harvesters	Hay-Makers	Tractors	Motors
1977	--	94	2839	3481
1978	116	272	3723	4910
1979	371	575	4886	6210
1980	415	901	4206	7431
1981	385	1533	4379	7051
1982	410	1933	4500	7481
1983	601	2200	5927	10054
1984	700	2476	6002	10976
1985	1390	2800	6002	11300
1986	300	1600	6100	11566
1987	1000	2600	6233	12000
1988	1360	2900	6500	12600
Average Increase per year	12.33%	45%	11.36%	12.90%

Table 5.11: Production of NEFM.

2.3. Evaluation of NEFM's Production

The assessment of production is limited to the major products of NEFM,which include combine harvesters, hay-makers, tractors and engines produced by the tractor and farm machinery plants (see Table 5.11).

The tables show a rise in the production of tractors and engines. The production of combine harvesters and hay-makers was also increasing until 1987.[2] This drastic fall was primarily the result of a shortage of components imported from abroad which resulted in the production line of the combine harvesters, for instance, being halted for 6 months.

However, the evaluation of production alone does not fundamentally offer a comprehensive assessment of the production performance of the firm. To do so, a comparative analysis with other parameters is necessary. The first comparison concerns the utilisation rate of production capacities. This can indicate the degree of capability and effectiveness in the use by the firm of the imported technology.

	1980	1981	1982	1983	1984	1985	1986	1987	1988
Forecasted rate(%)	50	55	58	60	65	65	70	70	75
Achieved rate(%)	44	46	50	55	55	57	54	59	61

Table 5.12: A comparison between the forecasted and achieved rate utilisation of production capacity.

	1980	**1981**	**1982**	**1983**	**1984**	**1985**	**1986**	**1987**	**1988**
Workforce	5836	5927	6275	6562	6700	6736	6800	7212	7232
Overheads	221	230	241	285	340	380	385	419	440
Production	595	650	740	991	1056	1232	725	807	1168
Imports of raw Materials	280	300	300	465	485	550	444	450	546

Table 5.13: Major parameters in NEFM (in millions of dinars).

2.4. The utilisation rate of production capacity

Two conclusions may be drawn from Table 5.12.

i.   In 1988, after 15 years of experience, the rate of utlisation of production capacity is still around 60%. In spite of the increase in production shown by Table 5.2, it is clear that imported technology remains inefficiently used in NEFM. This can undoubtedly be accounted for by the low levels of qualification of local skills.

ii. The persistent gap between the forecasted and achieved production rate is also another indicator of the poor level of management expertise in this organisation.

However, even though existing physical potential is not being fully used, the workforce and labour overheads continue to increase.

	1980	**1988**	**Rate of interest(%)**
Total workforce	5,836	7,232	+23
Labour cost(kDA)	221,000	440,000	+99
Labour cost per worker(kDA)	37.87	60.84	+61
Production(KDA)	595,000	116,800	+95
Production per worker(kDA)	101.95	61.50	+58
Import of raw materials(kDA)	200,000	546,000	+173

Table 5.14: Other parameters in NEFM between 1980 and 1988.

3. A Presentation of Other Parameters

The labour cost, as shown in Table 5.14, represents around 30% of the total overheads. The increase in overheads, workforce and materials, is more significant than the increase of production, as shown in the figures.

The increasing globalisation and the significant pace of technological change in farm machinery and the heavy investment it requires, have led to an international concentration of firms through mergers and take-overs. However, the Algerian strategy was to develop a national farm machinery industry focused on the desire to integrate more than 50% of local components in a country where industrial, technological and scientific support is lacking. This has led to the construction of large and complex plants such as the tractors plant, designed to manufacture ten different end-products as well as the parts to be integrated in these end-products. The farm machinery plant was also designed to manufacture 33 different end-products. In both plants, various technologies are used by an underqualified and inexperienced workforce. As a result, and after two decades of operation, there is still within these plants considerable idle production capacity. The utilisation of the capacity of NEFM's plants was, in 1989, not higher than 60%. It declined considerably after 1989. The increase in production costs had been higher than the increase in production volume (+61% of increase per worker and +58% of increase in production per worker). Such a strategy based on technological dissimilarity, seems difficult to implement with success in a developing country such as Algeria, where local skill and experience are lacking. This conclusion is confirmed by the completion of a satisfactory rate of production capacity by small plants in which simple technology is utilised in the manufacture of trailers and trucks. Even within the farm machinery plant, the simple manufacturing process of hay-makers is better assimilated than combine-harvesters. Thus, the more highly integrated and complex the plants are in terms of both the physical dimension and the technologies used, the more difficult it is to run them efficiently. The incompatibility between the complexity of the technology used and the local environment, characterised by lack of indigenous skill and competence, can be increased by the acquisition of advanced technology. This has a negative consequence on the performance of organisations from developing countries and slows down their learning process.

This incompatibility and its negative impact on firms' performance and learning curve is aggravated by the structural organisation which is characterised by:

i.   the separation of complementary functions such as production and techniques or inventory and supplies;
ii. the existence of several levels of hierarchy and decision-making centres;
iii. the fragmentation of tasks such as methods and work organisation.

Notes

1 Similar to other industries marked by a strong external dependency in terms of inputs, components and machinery, along with production and capacity utilisation, declined considerably after 1989.
2 After 1989 the whole production of NEFM declined as a result of a drastic reduction in imports. This company is also being restructured in order to be privatised.

Chapter 6
The Organisational Frameworks of NEEI and NEFM

This chapter reviews the organisational framework adopted by NEEI and NEFM by making reference to the theory of organisations. It also examines their degree of appropriateness in successfully acquiring and implementing new technology.

NEEI and NEFM are both state-owned firms and hence, their objectives, strategy, organisational structure are determined by the Central Government. Before examining and analysing the key organisational features of both organisations, it is necessary to start with a presentation of the major characteristics of Algerian firms.

1. Key Features of State-owned Organisations in Algeria

State-owned organisations depend strongly upon Central Government. Their mission is to execute and implement the decisions made by the Central Plan in terms of investment, job creation, production and technological development.

As a consequence, the organisations are involved in running several diverse functions and specialisations, such as research, project investments, production and distribution. In addition to this important vertical integration discussed in Chapters 3, 4 and 5 and because of the lack of industrial experience and the poverty of the local environment, other activities such as subcontracting, housing construction and even provision of services such as gas and electricity have to be undertaken by the organisation itself. This has inevitably led to huge state-owned organisations with 100,000 to 200,000 employees, which are difficult to run efficiently.

State-owned firms depend on capital allocated to them by Central Government and are then subject to a reinforced control which takes place at the Ministry of Finance, Ministry of Planning[1] and the Ministry in charge of the sector (Ministry of Heavy Industry for NEEI and NEFM). This dependency, as suggested in Figure 6.1, very often leads to conflicts between these different institutions that impede the performance of state-owned companies.

Algerian state firms were, until 1989, run according to a scheme adopted in 1971 known as the 'Socialist Enterprise Reform' which gave to workers of all levels the right to participate in the management of plants as well as the organisations. This type of organisation was subject to considerable controversy and managers were increasingly suggesting that it should be discontinued.

2. The 'Socialist Enterprise Reform' of 1971

The 'Socialist Enterprise Reform' was essentially based on workers participation in the daily management and control of the plants and the organisation's activities. Each socialist enterprise was managed by three bodies: the Workers' Assembly, the permanent Specialised Committees and the Management Committee.

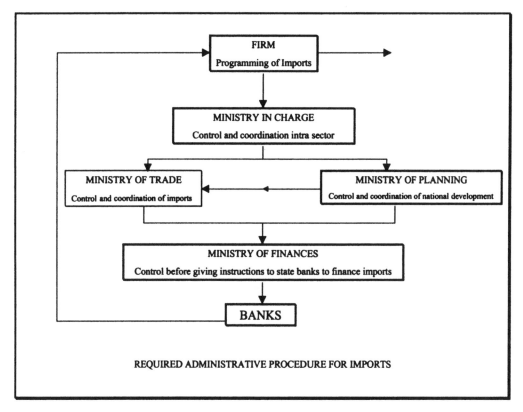

Figure 6.1: Administrative procedures for imports.

The Workers' Assembly was selected for three years and was accountable to the workers of the plant. Its real power was limited to the management of social activities and it did not hold any other decision-making power. There were five committees through which the Workers' Assembly participated in the daily management of their plants. These committees were:

1. Economic and Financial Committee
2. Social and Cultural Committee
3. Personnel and Training Committee
4. Disciplinary Committee
5. Health and Safety Committee

In committees (1) and (3), the workers were only given a consultative role. In committees (4) and (5), the power was balanced between the workers representatives and managers. Thus, complete decision-making power was restricted to social and leisure activities (committee 2).

The large majority of the members of the Management Committee were managers. The responsibilities of this committee were very broad, but only consultative. The

General Manager, appointed by the state, remained the main authority of this council. S/he made decisions on all important factors such as strategy, sales, production, stock inventory, expansion projects, investment programmes, budget, personnel. Workers, therefore, were not significantly empowered, they were just given a 'feeling' of power and encouraged through the committees to discuss how the plants and the organisation should be run. Managers, who were appointed by the Central Government and who were supposed to be qualified to perform these tasks, retained the sole rights, unassailable and guaranteed to manage both strategic and operational activities. However, little more than two decades after the adoption of this reform, the performance of Algerian state companies had not been satisfactory in terms of economic results or industrial relations. From 1969 to 1979, the deficit of state firms has increased by 348% and the utilisation of production capacity was not higher than 40%[2] Industrial disputes were also relatively high as shown in Tables 6.1 and 6.2.

A second reform known as the 'Restructuring of Firms' was adopted in 1980 in an attempt to overcome the major difficulties encountered by these state-owned companies.

3. The 'Restructuring of Firms' Reform

This reform was aimed at re-organising the structure of the state-owned organisations to enable them to improve their performance through greater specialisation and a significant increase of productivity. This implied a restructuring aimed at limiting activities to core specialisms and reducing their size. Another objective was to decentralise the process of decision. This was to be achieved by bringing decision-making centres nearer the production plants and by establishing autonomy within management.

It was anticipated that the specialisation focus would lead to significant increases in production and productivity through better utilisation of materials, human and financial resources and production capacity. Focusing on core activities would also

Year	1977	1978	1979	1980	1981	1982	1983	1984	1985
Number Of Disputes	189	188	260	420	487	476	424	475	360

Table 6.1: Industrial disputes from 1977 to 1985

Reason	1977	1978	1979	1980
Wages	34%	55.4%	66.7%	17%
Delay In Payment Of Wages	18.5%	-	-	38.5%
Working Conditions	11.6%	10%	2%	9%
Redundancies	15%	10%	14%	6%

Table 6.2: Main reasons for industrial disputes (%)

reduce the technological complexity and hence facilitate learning and continuous performance improvements.

The 'Restructuring Reform' was also aimed at improving the financial situation of state firms. The plan was that by 1985, most firms should have increased their rate of capacity utilisation to as much as 90%. This meant a 30–40% rise from the 1980 figures. This increase of productivity was to be achieved through an increase in production as well as a reduction of operation costs. The 'Restructuring Reform' was also supposed to enable state firms to significantly reduce overheads and production costs by, for example, decreasing the level of imported material stocks to a maximum of three months production and not filling job vacancies in order to reduce the labour costs.

The implementation of the 'Restructuring Reform' led to the creation of new organisations on the basis of the following criteria:

i.   specialisation in functions such as development, project management, production and distribution;

ii.   vertical structures and ownership of production and distribution activities;

iii.   regional firms to specialise in particular production-line systems and be given ownership of production and distribution activities.

The 'Restructuring Reform', built on the principles of rationalising the use of resources, imposed a shift from extensive to intensive type(s) of development, which did not require substantial additional investment. This reform has, however, led to a proliferation of firms and to an overlapping of competencies. The autonomy of state firms has simply not been dealt with since the state firm remains under the complete control of the central authority.

In spite of the 'Restructuring Reform', the Algerian state company is still seriously characterised by a high division of labour, a strong specialisation and differentiation between the functions. In addition, and as shown in Table 6.3, the authority pattern follows a pyramid structure with heavy control existing at all levels.

4. Impact of These Reforms on the Management and Performance of NEEI and NEFM

Since their creation in the 1980s, both firms have changed their organisational structures three times. The motivation for these changes was to some extent similar since the decision to modify the organisational structures came from the responsible

Levels	Managers	Workers representatives
Central Management	General Manager	Management Committee
Central Management	Functional Managers	Specialised Committee
Plant Management	Plant Manager	Management Committee
Plant Management	Functional Managers	Specialised Committee
Plant Management	Departmental Managers	Workers Assembly
Shopfloor Level	WORKERS WORKERS WORKERS	

Table 6.3: Levels of hierarchy existing in the 1971 reform.

ministry, the Ministry of Heavy Industry, who recognised the need to improve the flow between the different decision-making centres.

4.1. Organisational Structure of NEEI

The organisational structure up until 1987 was based on the following separation of functions:

i.   investments;
ii.   personnel and training;
iii. finance and accounting;
iv. technical;
v.   supplies and sales;
vi. planning, management and control;
vii. administration.

In 1987, the functions of personnel and administration were integrated into a new department given charge of the management of human resources. This 1987 re-structure also gave more importance to the major functions of the firm, the operations, development and commercial activities. The organisation was now divided into:

1.   Operational division with the following departments:
     i.   commercial department;
     ii.   development department;
     iii. operations department.
2.   Functional division with the following departments:
     i.   finance and accounting department,
     ii.   programming and systems department,
     iii. department of human resources.

At the beginning of 1990, a new organisational structure was introduced in which the separation between the operational and functional divisions was strengthened. Emphasis was now clearly placed on production activities. The operational division was meant to re-assemble all technical activities related to manufacturing. However, the commercial function responsible for sales, supplies and inventories was now separate from the manufacturing sphere. The operational division in charge of essential production activities was divided into the following divisions:

i.   production of audio goods;
ii.   production of video goods;
iii. production of industrial electronic goods;
iv. production of components kits;
v.   R&D.

The functional authority was responsible for the following departments:

i.   finance and accounting;
ii.   programming and systems,
iii. human resources,

iv.   commercial activities.

4.2. *Organisational Structure of NEFM*

The organisational structure up until 1987, was divided into eight different functions:

i.   administration;
ii.   technical;
iii.   production;
iv.   personnel and training;
v.   commercial;
vi.   programming and control;
vii.   development;
viii. finance and accounting.

This division and separation of functions was intensified in the 1987 organisational structure because the commercial department was subdivided into departments for local distribution and for imports and exports. The development department was also spilt into a development and project department and a department in charge of research. The second organisational structure includes the following departments:

i.   administration;
ii.   technical;
iii.   development and project management;
iv.   finances and accounting;
v.   imports and exports;
vi.   programming and audit;
vii.   personnel and training;
viii. local distribution;
xi.   research.

The third structure adopted in 1990 emphasised the separation of operational and functional authority with more importance placed upon the operational authority – as also observed in NEEI. This operational authority, responsible for the entire sphere of manufacturing activities, was divided into the following divisions:

i.   commercial, responsible for sales, supplies and inventories;
ii.   production of harvesting machinery and tractors;
iii.   production of agricultural transport and other farm machinery.

The functional authority was divided only into two departments:

i.   general administration, responsible for the co-ordination of personnel, training, finance, accounting and programming;
ii.   research and the co-ordination of development activities carried out in all the divisions.

The specialisation and separation of functions, in the 1990 organisational structure, was not as significant as it was in the previous structures. The motivation behind this organisational change is essentially explained by the need to integrate structures which are responsible for the same activities or which are producing the same product thereby enabling an easier exchange information.

4.3. *Analysis of the Organisational Structures of Production Plants*

There are in both companies six different levels of hierarchy:

    i.   general plant management;
   ii.   specialised area management;
   ii.   departments;
  iii.   services or workshops;
   iv.   sections;
    v.   groups.

The activities of the operational structures such as workshops, sections and groups are co-ordinated at the level of departments and specialised area management. Their organisation is essentially a product-line process and co-ordination is through formal procedures. This heavy reliance on formal procedures leads very often to a proliferation of decision-making centres and effective co-ordination is extremely difficult to achieve. It also creates a heavy and long flow of information which inevitably causes delays in the execution of tasks. As shown in Table 6.4, the number of levels of hierarchy has significantly increased through the different organisational reforms resulting in even more bureaucracy.

The major functions or specialised areas of these plants are very fragmented. The manufacturing function is divided into several departments, each of which are different decision-making centres. The Methods and the Organisation Department in charge of identifying the 'best way' for the workers to complete their tasks, are neither integrated nor centralised. Each workshop has its own office of methods and another office responsible for the organisation of work. The splitting of this major activity has led systematically to incoherence in planning, bad co-ordination and delays in execution of tasks.

Hierarchical Levels	First Chart	1987 Chart
Functional Management	4	8
Departments	4	22
Services or Workshops	24	75
Sections	84	135
Groups	72	231
TOTAL	188	476

Table 6.4: Evolution of levels of hierarchy.

The 1980 reform aimed at increasing productivity and overall performance through differentiation and specialisation led to a proliferation of decision-making centres which were often difficult to co-ordinate especially, for complex systems of technology and vertical integration. There was perhaps an attempt to group and integrate similar activities at central management level but this approach was not successfully applied at the manufacturing and operational levels.

The description of the organisational arrangements currently in operation in NEEI and NEFM correspond to what the literature describes as traditional or the Fordist model of organisation which is described in the next section.

5. Theoretical Analysis of Organisational Choices Adopted by NEEI and NEFM

The previous section has highlighted that the organisational arrangements currently used by Algerian state firms are largely influenced by the philosophy of Scientific Management. This section proposes to investigate the theoretical principles of the different organisational approaches used by these companies.

It emerges from the review of major organisational arrangements that state firms are strongly dependent upon the government and are executing policies decided by the state. The Central Plan determines in advance the volume of production and the necessary supplies. Wages are fixed within a national scheme according to qualifications and responsibilities. Investments are decided by the Central Government and tightly controlled by state banks. As state-owned companies benefit from a monopoly in their respective areas, they do not face competition and do not have to be attentive to market requirements. The management and organisational procedures are set by the ministry in charge.

All this limits initiative and may encourage state organisations to believe that they are operating in a predictable and stable environment. Perrow (1970) and Burns and Stalker (1961) suggest that organisations operating in this sort of environment tend to use routine technologies and a mechanistic structure. A mechanistic structure is defined by Max Weber (1984) as a bureaucratic type of structure, characterised by a clear hierarchy and involving strict specialisation and vertical communication. Indeed the analysis of the organisational charts used in both companies highlighted a structure characterised by:

i.   division of work and specialisation;
ii.   rigid separation of mental work from manual work;
iii.   fragmentation of tasks;
iv.   repetitive tasks;
v.   differentiation between functions resulting in strong boundaries between departments or groups involved in similar activities (production, methods, quality, maintenance, supplies);
vi.   clear lines of authority from top to bottom;
vii.   a pyramid hierarchy;
viii.   vertical communication;

ix.   salaries aligned to production.

It is notable that these principles are strongly advocated by Fordism.

The 'Restructuring Reform' aimed at improving the performance of state firms, was essentially reinforcing the principles on specialisation and division of work. This was justified by the belief that specialisation, fragmentation and the repetition of tasks facilitate learning in poorly skilled and qualified workforce. However, this restructuring has led to a proliferation of decision-making centres and to an overlapping of competencies. This is clearly illustrated in Table 6.4 where the number of hierarchical levels in the tractor plant has increased from 188 to 476!

On the other hand, the 'Socialist Enterprise Reform' set out to define the management procedures and organisational framework for Algerian state-owned companies. This reform demanded that workers participate in the management and control at both plant and organisational levels. The idea was to ensure employees involvement and commitment, through participation in responsibility and control, in order to establish, as suggested by Elton Mayo (1933), a necessary co-operation and consultation between workers and managers. This would ensure the workers' commitment and involvement through the satisfaction of his/her needs of initiative, responsibility and self-actualisation (Argyris, 1980; Coulson-Thomas, 1997). However, this participation is not free of controversy. Indeed the nature of areas where workers' representatives are responsible suggests an underlying objective of excluding them from other areas perceived as vital to the administration of the firms. The workers were therefore not treated as responsible. They were not significantly empowered but are just given a feeling of power. The analysis of this workers' participation has shown that the fact that the only responsibilities given to workers were the distribution of profits and the management of social and leisure activities. Workers' representatives were in parity with managers in the Health and Safety Committee and in the Disciplinary Committee. Consequently, key committees responsible for finance, economy and personnel were under management control. As responsibility was given to workers in areas believed to be of secondary importance, research has indicated that the 1971 Reform was based on the underlying idea that knowledge and expertise related to key activities such as production, sales, purchasing and investment are possessed only by managers. This seems to correspond to the underlying principle of division of labour featured in Scientific Management.

This division of work and separation between mental and manual work also explains the total lack of participation of workers in the management of operations on the production line. Here workers, as strongly advocated by Scientific Management, were simply executing tasks set and defined by managers. This kind of participation, instead of fulfilling the employees' needs of self-responsibility and initiative, has created frustration, evidenced by the large number of industrial disputes (shown in Table 6.1) and a high level of absenteeism.

In addition, granting the workers responsibility for profit distribution demonstrates that financial reward was still considered as a major motivator by the Socialist Enterprise Reform. Although the concept of 'social man', as defined by the Human

Relations School of thought, was included in the 1971 reform, the concept of 'economic man', advocated by Scientific Management , strongly underlies its philosophy. This dominance could be interpreted as undermining the commitment and the involvement of workers and therefore partly responsible for the low performance of both firms.

Where individuals are not allowed to take initiative or responsibility, the workforce becomes frustrated; high labour turnover and absenteeism result. In an attempt to overcome such a situation, the Central Government decided to introduce 'Financial Incentives'. These were to be related to both collective and individual performance measured against pre-established work goals. However, for simplistic reasons these 'Financial Incentives' were only related to production volume. Other parameters, such as quality of work and involvement, were found to be difficult to appraise. Indeed programmes where managers identify performance-related employee behaviour and then set a strategy to reinforce desirable behaviour and weaken undesirable behaviour have never been used nor even considered. This has led to further intensify the idea of 'economic man'.

The organisational arrangements currently used in Algerian state companies are increasingly characterised by homogeneity or, as named by Glover *et al.* (1983), a 'sameness' of situations and individuals. All Algerian state organisations have been subjected to the same organisational reforms set at a national level. Part of the New Personnel Regulations that were introduced, for instance, set predetermined wages for workers according to qualifications and responsibilities. This has created a tendency to generalise about both organisations' and employees' behaviour, ignoring any differences. It has been assumed that organisations and people will respond in the same way to a set of conditions. This is contrary to the modern 'contingency approach' that believes that there is no single 'best way', rather there are likely to be several different and acceptable behaviours or responses.

Also, these New Personnel Regulations have, in placing an emphasis on vertical rather than horizontal promotion, favoured bureaucracy rather than experience and stability. This is detrimental for engineers who seek promotion. They now have no alternative but to climb the ladder of vertical hierarchy taking on increasing administrative responsibilities.

In the current organisational structures of NEEI and NEFM, the creation of 'mega' departments, renamed "divisions", has happened through the integration of functions involved in the same domain. For example, the Commercial Division, Development Division and Operations Division have been created. Although limited to the level of central management, this reveals an attempt to reorganise the existing interface so that information is quickly exchanged and processed. Galbraith (1973) suggests that in a complex environment there is a need to develop information processing via a lateral communications flow. Lawrence and Lorsch (1967) go further and suggest that this integration of functions also serves the overall organisational goals by diminishing boundaries allowing for a better match between people and the imported technology, hence improving performance.

There appears to be a degree of awareness for the need to improve the communication flow between functions in other activities. The organisational structures used in NEEI and in NEFM show the integration of activities related to production (work organisation, scheduling, methods and maintenance). However, quality is perceived as a separate activity and the integration does not include activities, such as supply, inventory, design and selling, which are also very much involved in the conversion of inputs into outputs process.

Major features Of NEEI's and NEFM's organisational choice	Theory of organisation
Division of work Money is the main motivator Pyramidal authority Specialisation Bureaucracy Fragmentation of task Repetition of tasks Wages aligned to production Vertical communication Line of authority from top to bottom Separation between manual and mental work Strong boundaries between departments of groups involved in similar activities	Scientific Management
Limited participation of worker to management Attempt of goal-setting programmes via rewarding individual and collective performance	Human Approach
Attempt to take into account interaction between functions involved in similar activities Need to improve flow of communications	Systems Approach

Table 6.5: Presentation of NEEI's and NEFM's organisational choice with references to the theory of organisation.

The chief concern remains that integration is only taking place at the strategic level and not at the operational level. Here the functions remain all-powerful. This makes co-ordination of activities related to production extremely difficult to accomplish and leads to bottlenecks, large inventories, delays and ineffective use of resources.

The study of the two Algerian state companies with reference to the theory of organisations suggests a significant influence of Fordism in the way they organise and manage their business. Workers are viewed as incapable of taking responsibility. This contradicts the philosophy of the Socialist Enterprise Reform whose aim was to provide workers with a better life, inside and outside the workplace. This better life was supposed to be achieved not only by financial rewards but by better training and strong participation in the overall management of the organisation. However, most of the actions taken so far have been reliant on the use of financial rewards and decisions have been based on the assumption of the homogeneity of individuals and situations.

Table 6.5 compares and summarises organisational theory with the organisational arrangements of the Algerian state-owned firms.

The lack of contingency approach and the limited use of the systems approach can be explained by the poor level of indigenous capability in managing the process of technology transfer. Key features such as good internal communication, overall organisational approach and the quality and commitment of the workforce, which are vital for successful implementation of innovation, seem also to be lacking within both firms under study.

Notes

1   This ministry does not exist any longer as part of the reforms aimed at restructuring and establishing a market economy.
2   Results of the decade 1968–79, published by the Ministry of Planning.

Chapter 7
The Learning Process in NEEI and NEFM

This chapter proposes to identify the pattern followed by the National Enterprise for Electronic Industry (NEEI) and the National Enterprise for Farm Machinery (NEFM) in the development of their technological capabilities and to determine if this has followed any model defined by the literature review.

The chapter is divided into two major sections. The first, which defines learning as the most influential element determining the success of technology transfer, investigates the various mechanisms of learning acquisition and their impact on the development of local capabilities. The second examines the strategy used by NEEI and NEFM to develop their technological capabilities with reference to the models described in the literature.

As already mentioned, technology has essentially been conceived of as 'hardware' or a commodity which can easily be traded or transferred. However, technology is a two-component variable element, consisting of an 'embodied' component or hardware and a 'disembodied' part or software. Without this latter component, defined as 'knowledge capital' by Rulagora (1981), or 'technological capability' by Bell (1982), the 'hardware' is useless. The magnitude of this second component (technological capability) is expanding with the use of new technology systems based on information technology.

1. Development of Local Technological Capabilities

For Barrow (1989), technological capabilities are a complex combination of scientific knowledge, engineering techniques, craft skills, tacit knowledge and the social relations that make technology work. Bell (1984) suggests that technological capability includes three elements:

i.   The knowledge necessary to specify and define new techniques. This knowledge is likely to be in explicit forms such as textbooks and design manuals, as well as in tacit forms, i.e. within skilled people. This element is a technical knowledge that is based on design, engineering and R&D skills.

ii.   A knowledge base which is likely to be embodied in people. This provides firms with the skills and expertise to take a set of specifications and transform these into a new product or the construction of new plant or to simply improve existing products, processes or facilities.

iii.   The third element, often neglected, is institutional in nature and comprises the intra-firm managerial and organisational capabilities needed to provide an environment generating effective technical change. In this third element Bell includes also the relationships between the user and the producer of a technology.

Technological capabilities encompass different types of knowledge, experience and social relations. Their best use is dependent on the knowledge, skills and attitudes and the type of environment available within and outside the firm. For these reasons, technology cannot be regarded as a commodity which can equally be used in environments having less knowledge, skill and experience than developed countries, and it cannot be passively consumed by users in developing countries.

In this context, Dahlman and Cortes (quoted by Barrow, 1989) have identified five major categories of capabilities enabling firms in developing countries to set up manufacture plants. These are:

i.   the ability to select the appropriate technology;
ii.   the ability to install and operate the selected technology;
iii.   the ability to operate, repair and maintain the installed manufacturing facilities;
iv.   the ability to adapt and improve equipment, raw materials and end-products;
v.   the ability to create new technology.

Most of the capabilities listed by Dahlman and Cortes are aimed at selecting the right technology and providing efficient plant operation. They are known as 'know-how'. However, the ability to make major adaptations either to the product or to the process, or to develop new products requires a greater understanding of the design and production process. This 'know-why' capability is often omitted in debates regarding technology transfer in developing countries. For this reason, several analysts (Bell, 1982; Katz, 1982; Stewart and James, 1982; Teubal, 1984) have roughly divided technological capabilities into two major groups.

1.   Manufacturing capabilities or know-how, required to use a technology in the manufacture of a product or in the operation of the process.
2.   Design capabilities or know-why based on a thorough understanding of the system used.

Two comments need to be raised in relation to this categorisation of technological capabilities. The ordering of the capabilities as described above should not be seen as implying stages of development. In line with the conclusions of Chapter 1 regarding the process of innovation, the case studies carried out by Lall (1982) on Indian firms, Dahlman *et al.* (1978) and Barrow (1989) on South Korean experience, and Teubal (1984) on Brazil exports, show that the process of developing capabilities is not a linear progression, nor is it always the case that one capability is a pre-requisite for the next. In practice there is an important overlap between the different types of technological capabilities. These capabilities defined as skill, knowledge and experience are acquired by individuals or organisations via a process of learning.

2. The Process of Learning

For Bell (1982,1984), learning refers to the various processes by which skill and knowledge are acquired by individuals or perhaps organisations. Katz (1984) and Teubal (1984) are more precise and suggest that the learning process within the firm relates to a whole series of activities such as manufacture and plant operation,

Type of Learning	Positive Impact	Negative Impact
Learning by operating or learning by doing	Improvement of execution of production tasks	Passive consumption of imported technology and passive role of users. Low impact on learning curve.
Learning by changing	Acquisition of knowledge and understanding of technology used. Acquisition of confidence in manipulating the imported technology	Limited to the execution of production tasks. It is based on observation which can be passive if local capability does not exist
Crude copying	Low cost activity. It can lead to simplification of imported technology.	Essentially limited to the development of 'know-how' and does not lead to the generation of new technology.
Adaptive copying	Accompanied by adaptation of product design to improve quality or marketability. It develops 'know-how' and is based on disembodied technology.	Costly and requires higher level of skill and greater depth of manufacturing experience.
Learning by exporting	It can arise from acquisition of 'know-how' and 'know-why'	Requires incorporation into the firm of a large number of professional and technical personnel of different specialities.
Training	It is the major source of technological capacity	Cost and time consuming. Success is reliant on strategy of learning. A production orientated form of training limits the development of technological capacity.
Hiring of foreign	Helps to complement the local technological capacity by adding the missing components of experience and knowledge	Costly. If this approach is mainly orientated to execution of production tasks, the impact on learning is not positive
Searching	Increases the knowledge-base	Time and cost consuming. Requires a high level of skill.

Table 7.1. A presentation of the major mechanisms of learning and their main impact on capabilities development.

investment or project execution, product design and R&D. It therefore includes the creation and the strengthening of the whole set of skills, that is engineering skills, process engineering skills, and production organisation and planning skills. For developing countries, learning is based partly on the experience of production, partly on importing ready-made knowledge from industrialised countries and partly on a deliberate process of investing in the creation of knowledge.

Various forms of learning are identified by the literature. A summary of their key features is outlined in Table 7.1.

These different learning mechanisms can be grouped into the following three categories.

1.	A process whereby acquisition of knowledge and skill depends largely on experience or 'learning-by-doing'. This process is often considered to be 'cost-free'.

2.	A process of acquiring skill and knowledge by mechanisms that depend on the allocation of resources such as training, hiring of experts and searching.

3.	A third group, based on Lall' s definition (1992) of learning in developing countries, is proposed by this research. This group is the result of an interaction of extensive experience and investment in knowledge creation. It concerns, essentially, the acquisition of a disembodied type of knowledge and is named 'learning by using'.

2.1   Learning-by-doing Mechanisms

A flow of experience is derived from doing production tasks. It is, therefore, one kind of feedback mechanism which increases understanding and enables individuals to improve their own execution of given production tasks. Emphasis is often put on the production capability and what is often acquired is passive consumption of imported technology. Dahlman *et al*. (1982) show in their case study analysis, that detailed information and understanding of how and why the methods work are ignored. This process is described as relatively passive and automatic in the sense that it will occur at some rate with the passage of time or with increasing accumulation output. The integrated packages of the 1970s oil boom which have led to the implementation of the electronics, the engine and tractor, and the farm machinery plants, illustrate this type of learning. It was planned that a specific period (4 to 5 years) of executing production tasks would necessarily lead to the acquisition of skill and knowledge. That idea was even strengthened by the product-in-hand contract whereby the plant was supposed to be run under guarantees of international specifications. It was therefore believed that while producing according to international standards in terms of quality and quantity, a certain level of technological capability was going to be acquired by the case study firms. In practice, more than a decade after their implementation, these plants are far from reaching international standards.

This illustration supports the idea put forward earlier regarding the passive consumption of the imported technology. This learning mechanism is in fact based upon observation and participation in the production tasks. However, observation can be passive and a plant can, for instance, run for years without generating any of this kind of understanding if imported technology is regarded as just a consumable item. In this case, there is hardly any learning. Indeed research in developed countries (such as Gold *et al*. (1980) as well as the work of Huq *et al.*, (1992, 1993) and Lall *et al*. (1994) in developing countries has convincingly demonstrated that passive forms of 'learning-by-doing' have in fact contributed very little to productivity growth. If a form of learning emerges, as in the case of the two Algerian firms, it occurs after a long period of trial and error. Thus, the concept of cost and time in the learning-by-doing mechanism ought to be reconsidered. In both firms under study, the low rate of capacity utilisation (60%), the high level of production stoppage either because of raw material shortage or maintenance, the high rate of scrap (30%), show how consuming this learning method is in terms of time and cost. The 'learning by doing' is not, as suggested by scholars, 'costless'. It has, in both firms under study, led to significant consumption in time and in cost.

Learning in production only occurs if there is a feedback of information, enabling an understanding of the production process, and a flow of information which can be used to improve the production system. Thus, perception of possible improvements depend essentially upon the prior availability of skills and knowledge to analyse and interpret the information generated. In this case, the generation of knowledge and understanding is acquired through mechanisms requiring a deliberate allocation of resources. Along the same lines, Bell *et al.* (1984) argue that firms cannot rely on this type of learning in order to develop their technological capacities, and must invest in training and other knowledge creation.

2.2. Mechanisms of Learning Requiring Allocation of Resources

There are four main mechanisms through which skill and knowledge can be acquired in a process of technology transfer.

2.2.1. Learning through Training

Training is one of the most important sources of technological capacity. It can lead to the effective absorption of imported technical knowledge through various forms of training which may be incorporated into transfer arrangements. These may take the form of education in technical principles or training in the skills and expertise required to manipulate the imported technology. However, most developing countries have, as shown in the Algerian experience, been essentially orientated towards the execution of production tasks. There are nevertheless cases, based on learning by hiring, such as the Indian firm, Hindustan Machine Tools, which are discussed in the next section.

2.2.2. Learning by Hiring Experts

'Learning by hiring experts' is sometimes considered necessary to add important components of experience and knowledge to the local technological capacity. This form of learning has been very significantly integrated to contracts of technology transfer. Its impact seems to be linked to the type of contract adopted. Mascarenhas (1982) describes in great detail the experience of technology transfer via a joint venture between the Indian public sector enterprise Hindustan Machine Tool and the Swiss firm Oerlikans. She argues that this joint venture is acclaimed by all as having laid the foundations of the machine tool industry in India, especially because of the collaborator's emphasis on training. In this project the Oerlikans team, for instance, was responsible for training in: complete project planning, the selection, supply, erection and commissioning of plant machinery and equipment, the planning of the organisation and the setting up of procedures and systems. In addition to this extended training, aimed at acquiring the three elements of technological capability as described by Bell and discussed above, the starting up and running of production and management in all areas were supervised by Swiss experts. Barrow (1989) also claims that joint-ventures contracts have led to satisfactory 'learning by hiring' in countries such as South Korea. In Latin American countries, the 'decomposed' contract under supervision of hired experts seems to have resulted in the transfer of a sufficient level of technology capacity. In the case of the two Algerian firms under study, however, the 'product-in-hand' contract ceded the foreign experts complete responsibility for both the conception, execution and even initial management operation. There was hardly any local management participation in the project implementation and as a result, learning was not as positive as initially designed. It therefore seems that this form of learning is only effective when it is used to complement and strengthen the local technological capacity.

2.2.3. Learning by Searching

'Learning by searching' concerns the gathering of information about technologies which may not be acquired or which may only be acquired at a later stage. This mechanism increases the knowledge base on which future decisions about technological changes in product or production can be made. Thus, the success of this method depends on the effort made and the deployment of resources by the firm.

This aspect of learning is often neglected by firms in developing countries. In the two companies under study, the searching activities were quoted as a long-term preoccupation. Strong emphasis is still put on learning by operating with a dedicated investment in knowledge creation such as training.

The purpose of learning through allocation of resources is to provide prior skills and knowledge so that information generated by subsequent use of the production process can be analysed and interpreted in this way. This approach corresponds to the concept of learning consisting of a four-stage cycle: concrete experience, reflective observation, abstract conceptualisation and active experimentation.

This approach can help companies from developing countries avoid the passive consumption of the imported technology and move to another form of learning known as 'learning by using'.

2.2.4. Learning by Using

One of the basic purposes of 'learning by using' is to determine the optimal performance characteristics of equipment of a process. Such characteristics can often only be determined after a long period of use, many years in some cases. It is only through such extensive usage, that detailed knowledge is gained about product, process, maintenance needs and so forth. In 1987, eight years after its inauguration, the electronics plant had no stoppages because of maintenance problems. It is, therefore, a mechanism based on gradual learning combined with the interaction of experience and knowledge creation through allocation of resources. The knowledge generated in this way is described by Rosenberg (1982) as being of two forms: 'embodied' and 'disembodied'. The extensive use of equipment may, for instance, lead to the discovery of faults in components or design. This creates information considered as tacit knowledge, that eventually results in the physical modification of hardware which constitute the 'embodied' form of knowledge.

To assess this form of learning, this chapter analyses the evolution of parameters such as volume of output, quality, cost of production, maintenance and exports. Exporting is in practice more difficult than supplying the local market and could suggest a certain degree of learning through the need to achieve reasonable product quality, to produce more complex or sophisticated products, to understand users' needs or manage other factors such as long delivery times and supply of parts. The success of exports, as explained by Teubal (1984), in the case of Brazilian capital exports and Dahlman *et al.* (1987), in the case of South Korea, is the result of a learning process which is related to a whole series of activities (manufacture and plant operation, investment of project execution, product design and R&D) in which disembodied technology is vital.

3. Interactions between the Mechanisms of Learning and the Various Arrangements for Technology Transfer

After having described the different activities by which a firm can learn and the different mechanisms of technology transfer, the aim is now to analyse the different approaches undertaken by the two Algerian firms in the process of technology acquisition, and the impact of such approaches on their learning curves. The objective is to highlight whether a learning process is linked to any form of mechanism of technology transfer. As defined by Lamming and Bessant (1987), the learning curve represents the 'rate of progress made by an individual or organisation in acquiring new skills or absorbing new technological capability'. Empirical data gathered during visits to the case firms provides the basis for quantitative and qualitative analysis of the learning curve achieved by these two firms.

As mentioned earlier, most of the manufacturing capacities of the two companies being studied were set up during the 1970s oil boom through integrated contracts and in the 1980s through other forms of contracts, usually referred to as disintegrated or decomposed contracts.

3.1. Use of Integrated Contracts by NEEI and NEFM

The objective to be achieved through the integrated contracts, was to develop, in a relatively short period of time, electronics and farm machinery industries. As a consequence, the objectives of the electronics plant were reviewed in the sense of more vertical integration, with the maximum of guarantees to be provided by the outside partner. The guarantees concerned the economic and technical performance of the plant. The project cost was also reconsidered. The total increase was around 45% of the initial cost with an increase of 65% for technical assistance and only 13% for training and 6% for the equipment. The vertical integration implied the construction of large plants in which the whole process of production including the manufacture of all components and the assembly of end-products would be performed. The foreign partner was therefore required to deliver the following plants in working order.

1. Tractors and engines plant with 3446 employees – operational since 1974. This plant was designed to manufacture a range of 10 finished products.
2. Farm machinery plant with 1600 employees – operational since 1979. It was initially designed to manufacture a range of 33 different products and a wide range of components.
3. Electronics plant with 3429 employees – operational since 1979. The plant was designed to produce TV sets, radios, radio cassettes, music centres, car radios, TV aerials as well as a wide range of electronic components such as cathode ray tubes, capacitors, resistors, potentiometers, transistors, diodes, semi-conductors, integrated circuits, metallo-plastic pieces and TV cabinets.

Once again, the emphasis was essentially on developing capacities for operation of activities. The most important elements of management capability such as planning, organising, gathering and interpreting data to cope with changes were often neglected. This is evident from the orientation given to some of the learning mechanisms, based on allocation of resources such as training and technical assistance.

Training has not been disregarded since hundreds of Algerian students have been sent to the United States (partner of NEEI in the implementation of the electronics plant) and to West Germany (partner of NEFM in the implementation of the farm machinery plant and the engines and tractors plant). However, this training has mainly been carried out in a narrowly focused way aimed only at developing the level of skill necessary to operate the new technology.

Foreign assistance was also essentially devoted to operation activities. Dahmani's findings (1985) show that as much as 93% of the foreign experts in Algeria were allocated to operation activities, and just 7% to co-ordination, monitoring and organisation of production.

In addition to the above two points, the responsibility given to the technology supplier regarding the whole project implementation (design, construction, commissioning of facilities, provision of some skills, organisation structure and training inputs) has failed, as largely discussed in Chapter 3, to give local managers hands-on experience of project design and implementation.

3.2. *Impact of Integrated Contracts on Learning Curves*

As a consequence of the need to catch up as rapidly as possible, too much attention has been given to hardware acquisition by the two firms under study. Training has not been neglected, it has however, been carried out in a narrowly focused way aimed only at developing the minimum level of skill necessary to operate the new technology.

At the national level, institutions for training and for accumulating a national scientific and technological capacity have grown up but have not been able to keep pace with the level of technology imported and have not enabled Algerian firms to deal efficiently with its complexity. Indeed, Hoffman and Girvan (1990) report that in developing countries the contribution of science to improving the performance of industry has been minimal as a result of the very weak links between the science system and the production system. Consequently, the more complex the technology, the more contracts attempt to bring together all the project activities under the sole responsibility and co-ordination of the technology supplier. Thus, and as already mentioned in Chapter 3, such projects place greater emphasis on acquiring only the physical part or hardware component of technology.

This form of contract has failed to take into account other elements, such as complexity and compatibility. Local staff have not been involved and have therefore not undergone the development which participation in the project would have permitted and which might have allowed them to adapt and modify the imported technology according to the local requirements. A complex technology in an incompatible environment is unlikely to lead to progress in learning curves. As a result, managers and workers in local firms were not well equipped to analyse and interpret the feed-back provided by the execution of production tasks. The detailed information and understanding of how and why things work was simply ignored and was not viewed as an important element of the process of technology transfer. The lack of involvement of local managers in the initial phases of the project implementation, constitutes an obstacle to learning and to the acquisition of knowledge and understanding. Indeed Hoffman and Girvan (1990) argue that if local firms are 'denied these opportunities over a sufficiently long term period, such skills as do exist are going to be seriously under-utilised and will become marginalised from the production system'.

The dependence on outside assistance for management and skill operation is still significant. Difficulties such as breakdowns, delays in spare parts deliveries and repair facilities have, for instance, to be dealt with by foreign experts often located abroad. This leads to long delays in schedules and explains the chronic gaps between the designed and current utilisation of capacity and the designed and actual volumes of output.

This approach to the development of technological capabilities might be more successful in an environment already possessing a substantial level of skill, experience and knowledge and a national system to promote innovation and learning. However, and as shown in the following data, about half of the 60% of the workforce operating in production activities in these cases are illiterate.

The data in Tables 7.2, 7.3 and 7.4 also shows that considerable emphasis is placed on production activities with, for instance, most graduate and qualified people working in production.

This shows that what is typically sought is production capability but as the level of scrap and breakdowns and the gap between the forecast and the completed production are still substantial, it can be suggested that what is acquired is only the passive consumption of the imported technology. Detailed information and understanding of how and why the methods are ignored.

Dunning, quoted by Ebrahimpour and Schonberger (1984) argues that the important missing elements of the development in developing countries are the 'acquisition of knowledge, R&D techniques, production technology, and marketing and managerial skills'. What is therefore missing is the 'software' or the 'disembodied' component of technology. The experience of learning through the execution of

	Production	Technical Support To Production	Administration And Management
NEEI	67%	13%	20%
NEFM	62%	8%	30%

Table 7.2: Distribution of execution personnel.

	NEEI	NEFM
Production	71%	58%
Technical Support	10%	17%
Administration And Management	19%	24%

Table 7.3: Distribution of total workforce by activities.

	Graduates(%)	Technicians (A level)(%)	Execution(%)
NEEI	7.40	21.80	70.8
NEFM	3.60	16.40	80

Table 7.4: Distribution by category of workforce.

production tasks without the acquisition of knowledge and understanding constitutes a passive consumption of imported technology with very low impact on the development of in-house capabilities.

Production capability is presented by Dahlman *et al.* (op.cit) as comprising the following areas.

i.   Production management, which comprises the ability to plan, organise and improve the operations of existing plants.

ii.   Production engineering, which includes obtaining the information required to optimize operations.

iii.   Repair and maintenance.

These three elements correspond to the definition of 'know-how'. The 'know-why', based on a thorough understanding of the system used, is therefore ignored. In both firms, it was supposed that the integrated contracts would lead to the development of production tasks. However, as shown in the data related to the performance of NEEI and NEFM, both firms have been run for more than two decades without being able to approach the international management standards.

Learning by doing can generate an efficient production capability only if there is an in-house capability to gather and to analyse feedback of information. Capabilities in production management and production engineering depend essentially upon the prior availability of training and experience. For instance, it took about 15 years for NEEI to acquire a reasonable level of ability to plan, organise and improve the operations of existing plants. As pointed out by an engineering department manager, 'errors are still made and accepted, since it is the only way for us to learn'. This capability of gathering and analysing information has arisen in the two firms, and especially within NEEI, as a result of the interaction between the long process of 'learning by operating', and investment in training and recruitment of skilled people.

Thus, the turnkey contract, which is essentially based on 'learning by doing', has not provided the case-study firms with the production capability as defined above. It has been, rather, a passive consumption of imported technology. It is with the product-in-hand contract, by which provision of training and assistance are included as major elements, that a degree of progress along learning curve started within both firms. However, this learning curve effect was limited to the execution of production tasks. The non-involvement of local managers in the choice, purchase and installation of processes has not allowed their learning to include detailed information and understanding of how and why the methods work. As a consequence, parameters such as output and utilisation of capacity are not up to the level of the initial design. The cost of production is still significantly higher and the proportional increase of overheads to production is very large. Local managers are not involved in the pre-implementation phases of the process of technology transfer and consequently as Leonard-Barton (1988) and others argue local skills are not developed. Too much attention is still given to the acquisition of the hardware or the embodied component of technology. Training and hiring of experts have been used in the product-in-hand contract but have been limited to the minimum level of skills necessary to operate the imported technology. As summarised in Table 7.5, the emphasis in the two packaged contracts is placed on developing capabilities for the execution of production tasks.

4. New Mechanisms of Technology Transfer (Decomposed Contract) and Their Impact on Learning of NEEI and NEFM

In the early 1980s, both firms reconsidered their approach to technological development. This was essentially motivated by the following objectives:

i.   to accelerate the learning curve effect by ensuring greater participation of in-house staff in the whole process of project implementation;

ii.   to acquire better understanding of the technology used;

Major Objectives Of Turnkey Contract	Major Objectives Of Product-In-Hand
Conception and implementation of project	Conception, implementation, and initial management
Operation of the installed plant	Operation and initial management of the installed plant
Learning by doing	Learning by doing Learning by training Learning by hiring experts
Low execution of production tasks	A better execution of production tasks
Passive consumption of imported technology Emphasis placed on hardware	Acquisition of 'know-how' but limited to execution of production tasks

Table 7.5: Presentation of the major mechanisms of learning and their main impact on capabilities.

iii.   to achieve financial savings.

As a result of the improvement of their bargaining capability through information acquisition, diversification of partners and technical training programmes, the two Algerian firms felt motivated to divide up projects as much as possible to ensure their participation in the whole process of technology transfer. This led to a multiplication of contracts, partners and thus of responsibilities.

The objective of this unpackaged mechanism of technology transfer is to augment the technological capabilities of the firm while upgrading existing technology and implementing new projects. Technology suppliers are contracted to provide state-owned companies with technical documentation, technical assistance and supervision. By adopting a 'trial and error' approach in managing the following investment projects under supervision (technology supplier), both firms have developed a degree of expertise in project management capability:

1.   The audio plant, which has been in operation since 1986, took a year longer than planned to construct and the total cost was 70% higher than initially planned. The financial re-evaluation and the delay seem to show the low ability the firm has in planning and organising investment activities. Two major reasons are given by NEEI management to justify this re-evaluation:

   a.   A change of the physical configuration of the plant because of errors in planning at the level of the firm strategy. New objectives were allocated to the audio plant and the surface area of the plant was increased by 35%.

   b.   The area selected for this project construction was very poor and the firm had to take responsibility for providing services such as electricity, gas, water and housing for managers.

2..   The TV aerials plant has been in operation since 1986. This project was also one year over schedule and went through a re-evaluation in 1983, just one year after the initial studies. NEEI management considers that it was only at that date (1983), that organisation and planning activities of that specific investment were efficiently managed. For this reason, the financial cost was increased by 131%.

3.   Medical equipment plant. The trial and error approach adopted in the two above projects has enabled NEEI to gain experience in project management. As a consequence, the operation was launched as planned in October 1988 and the financial cost was not significantly increased (40%). The major reason for the financial re-evaluation was the devaluation of the local currency.

For the installation of these projects, NEEI under the supervision of foreign partners took over of the following activities:

   i.   civil engineering;
   ii.   engineering studies regarding equipment, process and lay-out;
   iii.   purchase of equipment based on mutual agreement;
   iv.   installation of equipment;
   v.   training – provided by NEEI training centre and completed on the site.

In projects carried out in the course of 1990, local managers and engineers were even involved with designing technical documentation and management systems. In this type of contract, local users were given the opportunity to participate in all the phases of the project: pre-investment, investment and post-investment. During the pre-investment phase, local managers were fully involved in the project feasibility which include activities such as:

i.   identification and definition of services and machinery needed for the project;
ii.   selection of the process and the supplier;
iii.   identification of the skill and expertise requirements and the training needed.

As Hoffman and Girvan (1990) report, the level of technical detail and hence skill and expertise (engineers, economists, technicians) required to accomplish such activities is quite high and is provided by foreign consultants, who in the context of a decomposed and supervised mechanism of technology transfer, are assisted by local users.

When a decision to proceed with a project is taken, the second phase or investment begins whereby detailed information related to installation and operation of the selected process is collected. The phase ends with the construction of the plant and installation of equipment. The last or post-investment phase refers to the full operation of the plant. As already pointed out, a greater and earlier involvement of local users in project management is more likely to increase the level of local technological capabilities and lead to an effective management of the post-investment or operational phase.

The empirical data shows the development of skill and expertise in project management achieved by NEEI as a consequence of the participation of its managers under supervision of foreign partners, throughout the whole process of project implementation. This learning curve is also the result of the long 'learning by doing' experienced by the firm and the impact of investment in training and in recruiting graduates and skilled workforce.

As a consequence of this participation of local managers and the type of learning which was used, the audio and aerial plants were brought up to 70% of capacity utilisation after just two years of operation. A senior manager of NEEI stated that within the audio and aerial plants, production systems and maintenance were fully under the control of local skill by the end of 1987, after two years of operation.

It took, however, a decade for the plants installed through integrated contracts, to reach such a rate. For the electronic plant installed through integrated contract and in operation since 1979, poor maintenance was, until 1987, the main reason for production stoppages.

This form of contract based on unpacking and foreign supervision has also enabled both firms, with the collaboration of foreign partners, to achieve technological adaptations of components and end products. These modifications have led to savings in energy and raw materials consumption. In NEEI, successful modifications have been carried out in printed circuit boards, cathodic ray tubes and metallo-plastic pieces. NEFM has also carried out simple but successful adaptations of tractors and combine harvesters to satisfy local requirements and specificities. These technical changes have mostly been achieved as the result of the use of the reverse engineering method and copying.

Imitation and copying constitute another approach used by both firms to develop their capabilities. NEEI and NEFM both started as repair and maintenance shops and have used the reverse engineering method to gain a better understanding about the process and the equipment used, their functioning, and their optimal performance characteristics. Tractors and combine harvesters have, for instance, been disassembled in order to identify their design and process principles and the full set of specifications they incorporate. This reverse engineering process has also allowed NEFM to determine material specifications used in their production.

Both firms have also attempted to integrate local components in their manufacturing process. Their objective was to substitute as many of the imported components by local ones as possible. Figures given by both firms show a satisfactory rate of local integration.

black and white TV set	80%
colour TV:	35%
tractor	60%
combine harvester	68%
engines	70%

It appears, however, that this integration has essentially concentrated on the peripheral, low-tech parts of the finished product (iron, aluminium, painting, plastic). It is therefore inappropriate to interpret these figures as indicating high levels of learning about the processes used.

The decomposed contract has also led to an alteration of cost distribution of projects. For the audio plant, 75% of the total cost was spent on equipment and 95% of this equipment was of standard type. The remaining 5% was allocated to non-standard equipment. Emphasis has been placed on generic equipment so that the understanding of its principles, the determination of its performance characteristics and its maintenance can easily be achieved. The switch from specific to generic equipment is also motivated by the need to acquire machines that can be used for different purposes. This shows a desire for a shift from mass production organisation based on the use of very specific machinery to a form of flexibility in the use of production facilities. This endeavour can be interpreted as a sign of awareness of a need for organisational change to enhance performance.

This new strategy of implementation of new technology was therefore aimed at providing the two firms with capabilities to deal with change and to manage investment projects. Dahlman *et al.* (1987) call these 'investment capabilities' and include the following elements.

i.   Organisation and planning of investment activities in the case, for instance, of installation or expansion of new facilities.

ii.   Project engineering which provides the information needed to make technology operational once installed.

Thus, the major approach for developing investment capability is to take part in the whole process of expansion or installation of plants in order to secure some capabilities from each phase of the investment process. By performing some or most of investment project tasks, managers from developing countries can gain and accumulate a good level of details and understanding about investment as well as production capabilities. As shown in the Brazilian (Teubal, 1984), Korean (Barrow, 1989 and others) and Indian (Lall, 1982) experiences, more information and understanding with respect to the functioning of the plants is gained by participating throughout the phases of an investment operation. Along the same line, Hoffman and Girvan (1990) claim that 'learning by doing may merge into more explicit forms of training when projects incorporate participation of individuals and organisation ...'. This participation is effective when components of experience and knowledge can be added to the technological capacity through training and education, research and hiring of foreign experts. Thus, augmenting the investment capability seems to depend upon a combined set of learning mechanisms. In addition to training, investment in R&D have provided both firms with the capacity to carry out technological changes such as modification of electronic components and farm machinery end-products, imports substitution and integration of local components.

The various mechanisms of learning used by NEEI and NEFM and the different arrangements of technology transfer adopted, have allowed the two firms to seek the optimal performance characteristics of the technology process implemented. The use and the interactions of the various forms of learning have led to an accumulation of detailed knowledge about the technology system used. This form of learning is categorised as 'learning by using' and it is essentially of disembodied form as suggested by Rosenberg (1979). The acquisition of this disembodied part of technology has generated capabilities to undertake and manage technological changes in products and processes as shown in the examples discussed above.

In addition, both firms have, as a result of the adoption of various mechanisms of technology transfer and the different process of learning implemented, started developing capabilities in the course of managing changes in procedures and organisation arrangements.

5. Organisational Reforms and Development of Management Capabilities

A series of organisational reforms have been introduced in order to enhance performance through better use of resources and management capabilities.

5.1. The Restructuring Reform

One of the first impacts of this reform was to reduce the size of the larger plants through a cutback of their vertical integration. The manufacturing range of the farm machinery plant was reduced from 33 different products to just 4, i.e. combine harvesters, hay-makers, mechanical harrows, and mechanical grass cutters. The others were transferred to the firms' other plants.

The purpose of this change was to increase the volume of output by a better use of production capacities and to develop subcontracting activities. As a result of the changes, the output of both firms went up. This trend was, however, drastically affected by the drop of oil prices (1986 and 1987). Both firms were unable to get adequate credits to finance their supply needs. Despite the relatively high level of integration of local components achieved in the production process, NEEI and NEFM remained entirely dependent for their supplies on foreign companies as suggested by the following ratios comparing the supplies from abroad to the total supplies of NEFM (see Table 7.6).

This dependence is even higher in the electronic firm. For this reason, both firms have not been able to maintain their production activities at an adequate level. This, seems to support the earlier assumptions about the essentially peripheral nature of the substitution level that had been achieved. The drastic decrease of 1987 and the heavy dependence of both firms on supplies from abroad may also be explained by the adoption of vertical integration in plants with low level of knowledge, experience and subcontracting support.

The level of stock of raw materials is as high as 7 months of production in NEEI and 11 months in NEFM. The scrap rate in both firms is around 25% and the utilisation of production capacities is not higher than 60%. The cost of production is still quite high as a consequence of the heavy overheads existing in both firms. In NEEI for instance, where the overall performance is better than NEFM, the increase of the total overheads from 1982 to 1986, was 80%. For the same period, the increase of the production output was not more than 50%.

It appears from the interviews with managers and engineers of both firms that their learning and more particularly their learning in management has been considerably obstructed by their strong dependence on governmental bodies. As shown in Figure 6.1, a firm has first to report to the ministry in charge of its industry (Ministry of Heavy Industry), to the Ministries of Planning and Finance for its investment activities and to the Ministry of Trade for its import and export activities. The lack of autonomy has in fact not been overcome by the 1980 restructuring reform and it still acts as an obstacle to motivation and development of managerial capabilities.

The second reform implemented in 1989 was supposed to provide Algerian managers with the possibility of promoting initiative and effectiveness and to augment their management capability.

1980	1981	1982	1983	1984	1985	1986	1987	1988
88%	89%	84%	84%	81%	79%	61%	66%	76%

Table 7.6: The percentage of foreign-based supply.

5.2. Autonomy Reform

This reform's main objective was to give to enterprises complete autonomy in order to promote initiative, coherence and integration in their management approach and to consider the market as the major regulator instead of the central plan. The essence of this reform was similar to the restructuring reform since the objectives were still considered as:

i.   increasing productivity by the efficient use of existing production capacity;
ii.   stimulating innovation;
iii.   enhancing the valuation of the work by employees;
iv.   responding very quickly to new market needs;
v.   improving performance and competitiveness.

The solutions are still to do with enterprise autonomy, management initiative and stronger market orientation. This, can be considered as a response to the independent attitude developed by Algerian managers. There are in fact several cases confirming this suggestion, where managers have simply crossed the rigid boundaries of legislation to be more innovative.

NEFM has, for instance, launched a scheme by which workers were given material and financial support to develop subcontracting activities thereby relieving itself of secondary activities. The objective of this scheme was to enable NEFM to focus on core activities and to outsource as many secondary activities as possible. The company was also aiming at reducing its strong dependency on foreign suppliers and was creating a pool of reliable suppliers with whom the company was intending to establish a stable and long-term relationship. They also sought by this initiative to reduce the number of employees.

Within the electronic plant at Sidi-Belabes, a production engineer has successfully implemented the technique of quality circles. This technique has allowed the wire-winding workshop to reduce the scrap rate from 30% in 1985 to 20% in 1987 and to 15% in 1988. The technique has also improved the workers' motivation significantly as well as the relationships within the hierarchy of the plant as a whole. Absenteeism has gone down in NEEI to 5.65%, compared to 7.68% in NEFM. The approach was, however, limited only to wire-winding workshop.

These examples and the analysis of the development of capabilities experienced by the firms under study suggest that optimal use of imported technology is also highly subordinated to the development of managerial and organisational capabilities, that is involvement in techno-managerial activities associated with investment as well as operations activities. These capabilities are reliant on the acquisition of a disembodied component of technology that Bell (1986) has identified as an element of knowledge which is institutional in nature and which consists of both the intra-firm managerial and organisational capabilities and the inter-firm relationships. However, studies in developed countries (Simmonds and Senker, 1989) have pointed out the difficulty of securing such learning in firms already holding a high level of skill, expertise and experience and familiar with the use of advanced manufacturing technology (CAD, CAPM).

The learning curves within NEEI and NEFM, followed to some extent, the same pattern. Learning started in these two firms with an attempt to develop the production capability through the execution of production tasks. This was made possible by the adoption of highly integrated packages of transfer of technology such as 'turnkey' and 'product in hand' contracts in which the role of the foreign contractor was very substantial and the involvement of local managers ignored. Consequently, the detailed information and understanding of how and why things work was not completely acquired. For this reason, learning within these two firms has been re-enforced by the use of decomposed contracts which has led to the deepening of the production capability through the acquisition of knowledge and information regarding the technology used. This new approach to technology transfer has also led to the development of investment capability as a result of a greater participation of local managers in the technology implementation. The local participation in the process of project investment has substantially increased the capacity to manage changes. And finally, by the mid-1980s, and with the development of an independent attitude of the managers, a third step of learning concerned with management ability has started to be developed. This attitude of the managers is mainly motivated by the need to use efficiently the imported technology so that the overall performance of the firms can be enhanced, and be more competitive in the international market.

It can therefore be concluded that the sequence of capabilities has followed a linear progression, as shown in Figure 7.1, however, with interfaces and feedback mechanisms between the different steps. The process has, for instance, to be reconsidered and re-started with the changes in mechanisms of technology transfer and the revision of objectives. This revision has, nevertheless, been possible because of learning achieved during previous experiences.

The described pattern of the learning curve of both firms is to some extent in line with the pattern suggested by Dahlman *et al.* except for the third step which he views as being included within the development of innovation capability. The innovation capability consists of creating and carrying new technical possibilities through to economic possibilities. These new technical possibilities can be divided into two different types of innovation.

i.   A radically new technology or a major innovation that can be developed either from basic research activities known as 'Push theory', or from an identification of a need for which a technical solution has to be found, i.e. 'Pull theory'.

ii.   A modification or improvement of existing technology known as minor innovation which is developed from applied research and development as well as a trial and error approach.

Most innovative activity in NEEI and NEFM as well as in most of the firms of the developing countries, is of the second type. Capabilities in both firms have essentially been generated through minor changes. These incremental innovations have, for instance, been developed with the need to adapt the imported technology, to integrate the local raw materials into the production system and especially with the need to use efficiently the implemented technology so that the firms' performance can be improved.

The 'innovative capability', does not therefore appear as such in the pattern of capabilities developed by the firms of the case study. Because of the low availability of skill and experience within these two firms, emphasis has always been placed on incremental and minor innovation activity. For this reason, it can be argued that the development of innovation capability seems to be a major component of each of the three steps identified in the case study analysis. Minor innovations, either in the form of physical changes or, in disembodied changes, were supposed to be carried out at each level of the learning pattern. The assimilation of the imported technology was for instance planned for 1980, and, the ability to modify and adapt was planned to be reached by 1985. The development of R&D work has, however, always been considered as a preoccupation for the years 2000. That is why, this study proposes the generation of major or radical innovation in a fourth step of capabilities development.

Similarly, the third step of management capabilities development identified in the process of learning of the firms under study is not considered by the Dahlman *et al.* (1987) study as a separate step. It seems to be present as an element generated at each

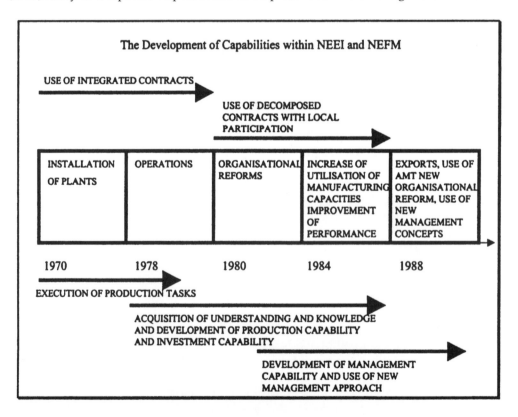

Figure 7.1: The development of capabilities within NEEI and NEFM.

step of development capabilities. The ability to plan, to organise, to improve the operations of existing plants and to organise and plan changes and investment activities, cannot be achieved unless the following conditions are set:

i.   availability of local technological capacity

ii.   acquisition of the disembodied component of technology.

These two conditions therefore explain the reasons for the appearance of the development of management capabilities within both firms in the mid-1980s and 1990s. The extensive execution of production tasks and the investment in knowledge creation have just started generating the need to acquire knowledge and understanding so the optimal use of technology can be obtained. The development of organisational and managerial capability has also coincided with the emergence within NEEI and NEFM of the need to purchase and use machines which can allow flexibility in production and the integration of similar activities in order to improve communication and hence overall performance.

The study of these Algerian experiences has shown the case of a developing country trying hard to acquire technological capabilities against a background of a strict state and bureaucratic control and a relatively low level of skills and qualification. In spite of substantial investments in advanced technology, the performance of the two state-owned organisations in terms of quality and quantity is still below expectations. More than a 20% reject rate and a 50% rate of capacity utilisation is recorded. Simply investing in technology is no guarantee of its success. Greater emphasis needs to be placed on effective and on-going learning. Organisation changes are also needed to gain the full potential of the new technology.

Chapter 8
Effective Acquisition of Technology through Organisational Changes

This chapter focuses on the necessity for companies from developing countries to undergo changes to methods of organisation that will enable the successful transfer and management of the new technology systems. It challenges the traditional, Fordist model of organisation and examines the necessity for developing new organisational arrangements aimed at improving overall performance rather than merely depending upon investment in physical equipment. It explores the possibility of organisations, from developing countries, enhancing their performance through new forms of organisation that can be simple to adopt and assimilate. It suggests a shift towards forms based on the participation of shopfloor workers, the commitment of managers and the gradual removal of the separation between the management and operation functions. The chapter is divided in four sections. The first describes the key features and the main determinant of advanced technology in industrialised countries. The second and third sections review the Algerian experience and highlight the main inhibitors to effective technology transfer in developing countries. The fourth section examines the nature and the underlying principles which form the basis of new forms of organisation known as 'Post-Fordism'.

Research on the use of advanced technology in developed countries, as well as in developing countries, has clearly highlighted that its effective acquisition and implementation is extremely reliant on changes in organisational approach and higher levels of in-house skills and competence. The traditional model of organisation designed to suit a predictable environment is no longer appropriate to a highly complex, competitive and global market place. To surmount this obstacle, Liu *et al*. (1990) advocate the need for change in order to achieve a good fit between new technology and organisation. This fit, which is more likely to create a greater compatibility and complementarity at both a micro- and macro-environmental level is perceived as a critical pre-requisite and major enabler for the development and diffusion of innovation.

The changes envisaged are primarily the outcome of the new tasks and roles allocated to workers in order to effectively use, monitor and maintain new machine tools based on a growing level of integrated technology. Increasing and rapid changes in market and customer needs are no longer associated with an organisational model designed for a predictable environment and market. Success is significantly linked to new organisational arrangements conducive to continuous innovation and learning in order to manage uncertainty and complexity in business.

1. Key Features and Diffusion of Advanced Technology in Developed Countries

This section aims to outline the key features of advanced technology which is also described as systems technology, and which is based on an increasing integration of computing, automation and communication technologies.

In the past, competition and business were essentially concerned with mass production in which, goods were delivered to customers in fairly constant volumes at fairly constant time intervals according to long-term schedules. The market was considered to be relatively predictable and competition was essentially price based on manufacturing goods at minimum cost. Thus, the performance of such manufacturing systems was mainly focused on rationalisation and reduction of labour costs in order to improve productivity. The situation has, however, changed and the firms are now dealing with continual fluctuations in which the key factor in competition has shifted from productivity alone to an overall responsiveness to changes in the market. Thus, survival in competition depends on reacting more flexibly and adapting more rapidly to customer requirements. This alteration means coming to terms with the idea of greater product and part diversification, higher quality demands and shorter product development and delivery periods. The emphasis is now put on the need to reduce lead times and to improve quality and responsiveness while maintaining low cost. To meet these new challenges, new technology systems have emerged and have led to new principles for production, organisation and management marked by less division of tasks and more integration of functions and activities.

1.1. Development of Advanced Technology

In line with the historical evolution of innovation introduced in Chapter 1, the development and diffusion of advanced technology has followed an evolutionary path which can be divided into three major phases as illustrated in Figure 8.1.

The first phase is mainly concerned with stand-alone-machine automation such as the NC machine tools developed in the early 1950s in the metalwork industry. It is a method of control that uses symbolically coded instructions to cause the machines to

PHASE 1	PHASE 2	PHASE 3
Single Applications	Integration of various functions	Intra- and inter organisational integration and networks

GREATER INTEGRATION.

⟶

Figure 8.1: Evolution of manufacturing technology.

perform a specific series of operations. When a job changes the program of instructions is also altered. In the late 1960s, as the result of the extensive development of the NC system, the control unit of the machine tool was replaced with a micro-computer. This has subsequently increased the level of flexibility since programs stored in the memory can be edited as necessary to accommodate design changes. Another key feature is the emergence of integrating different functions such as transport, loading and management. This new attribute has made necessary organisational and managerial adaptations in order to ensure a better use of this technology system.

The second phase is marked by the growing emergence of machine tools based on a combination and a greater integration of various functions and activities. This integration is regarded as the key alternative to the manufacturing activities of the 1980s with the successful utilisation of flexible manufacturing systems (FMS), computer aided design (CAD), computer aided manufacturing (CAM), CAD/CAM and robotics.

It appears from Table 8.1 that this new technology is not introduced purely for productivity improvements, but for a wider set of objectives. This suggests that new technology is rarely installed for a single motive. The most common justification for investing in new technology systems is the improvement which it brings to the overall performance of the company and to its image.

FMS	CAD
Productivity improvement	Lead time reduction in:
Consistency and quality	responding to customers
Better utilisation of equipment	making modifications
Lead time reduction in manufacturing	new product development
Shorter manufacturing cycle time	Productivity improvements
To handle a greater part variety	Less errors in design
Reduction in inventory levels and reduced material usage	Improved utilisation of raw materials
Less space for inventory and manufacturing	Consistency and quality
Decrease in scrap rate	Simulate and investigate alternative options
Changes to product mix	Improve overall image of the company
Consistent levels of output	
Easier shopfloor control	
Improved speed and quality of management information	
Improved control and reduced disruption	
Upstream and downstream of the FMS	
Ability to react quickly to changes	
Improved control over materials handling	
Improved company image	
Introduction of multi-skilled working	
To respond quickly to business needs	

Table 8.1: Benefits from new technology.

In the third phase this integration is extended beyond the boundaries of the firm through linkage between firms on design, purchasing and distribution. This pattern of integration systems and networks is increasingly blurring the boundaries between tasks, functions and areas within a firm and even between firms.

1.2. Main Determinants of the Diffusion of Advanced Technology in Developed Countries

The diffusion of this new technology seems to be reliant upon solid prerequisites. In a study carried out for The British Institute of Management by New and Myers (1986) of Cranfield Institute of Technology, users of advanced manufacturing technology were asked to rate their investments in terms of their views on the return to the firm. Their response indicated that 46% of CAD users, 70% of FMS users and 80% of robot users were dissatisfied. In another study of users of advanced manufacturing technology, Burns (1988) report that 9 out the 21 systems observed were performing below expectations and in four systems out of the 12 identified as satisfactory, 4 experienced long delays before the systems come up to expectations. Rush (1989) and Simmons and

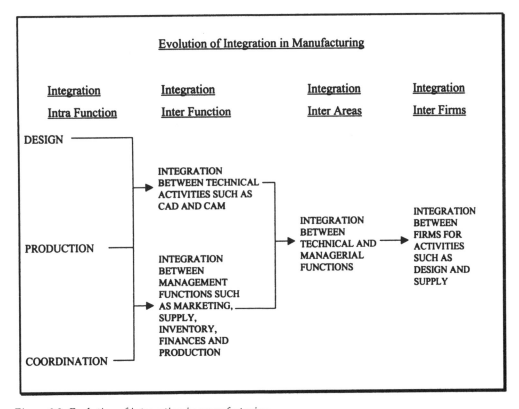

Figure 8.2: Evolution of integration in manufacturing.

Martin *et al* (1985) (CAD)	Foyer, UK Ingersol Engineers (1985) (FMS)	Works Management (CAPM)	Commission for Europe (FMS)
Efficient application Selecting the right system and fitting it within the entire business training at all levels.	Thorough business planning Sound reasons for investment Careful selection and management of people Planned and organised acquisition of information	Involvement of workforce at all levels Preparedness to change practices Education Selection of team members	Preparedness to achieve best practice in as short time as possible Involvement of management at all levels Involvement which should intervene at the planning stage Acquisition of knowledge and understanding about the system

Table 8.2: Key factors of successful innovation.

Senker (1989) argue that effective use of the advanced technology is essentially affected by skills, organisation and management.

Nicholas *et al.* (1983) and Simmonds and Senker (1989) provide evidence that new technology systems such as CNC, CAD and FMS have been more effective when implemented in conjunction with organisational and procedural adjustments. In the companies which were still structured according to Fordist principles formalised structures, activities and groups with a common objective were not merged and harmonised, and tended to be structurally isolated from each other. This affected the flow of information between departments and impeded the implementation of the new technology.

Another major constraint on the effective use of advanced technology, has been a lack of in-house skills and knowledge. The adoption of this new technology has introduced a trend towards the integration of the production system whereby the level of decision-making and information processing has increased, requiring a more skilled and qualified workforce. However, a report produced by the Institution of Production Engineers in 1985 pointed out that technological progress in Britain was inhibited by a failure to develop human resources to exploit new technology.

It was also claimed that obstructions to the efficient use of advanced technology such as CAD were generated by the lack of skill and awareness about the full potentialities of this advanced technology primarily at management and operation level (Arnolds, 1984; Simmonds and Senker, 1989; Bessant and Buckingham, 1991). This was echoed by a report of the Department of Employment (1988) stating that 'If the business is to be successful in the highly competitive world of the 1990s, management training, particularly for those already in management jobs, must move to the top of the agenda of every enterprise.'

There are, however, cases where firms have been able to implement successfully advanced and secure full benefits from this integrated technology as a result of supporting workforce learning at all levels and conducting simultaneous organisational adaptations (Coulson-Thomas, 1997).

The diffusion of advanced technology in industrialised countries substantiates the notion that successful implementation of technology does not depend on a single factor but rather on a multi-factor and holistic analysis. It suggests strongly that implementation does not only bring changes at the level of production but also to the whole business and as a consequence, it illustrates a new way of organisational and managerial approach that Bessant (1990) describes as 'post-Fordism'.

2. Major Features of the Process of Technology Transfer in NEEI and NEFM

In the previous chapters it was concluded that technology transfer in NEEI and NEFM had been limited, mostly to the physical aspect of the technology. This movement was characterised in both organisations by the considerable vertical integration that led to the construction of massive production plants based on complex combinations of dissimilar technologies. For NEEI and NEFM, this approach meant the assimilation of new techniques as diversified as:

i.   the integration of raw materials and sub-group production in the manufacturing process;
ii.   components and parts manufacturing;
iii. the design and development of new products;
iv.   changes to the assembly process and the testing of end-products.

Automation Magazine (CAPM)	Bessant (CAD)	Francis (CAD)	PSI Survey (AMT)
Lack of understanding of MRP2 Lack of education Lack of communication	Lack of understanding of systems Inappropriate background or no experience Inappropriate organisation	Inappropriate system for the task User fears leading to use of manual systems Learning curve investment Conflicts of interests between users and suppliers	Lack of expertise High costs Lack of capital Technical problems Difficulty with suppliers Resistance from workforce Resistance from managers

Table 8.3: Major obstacles to diffusion of advanced manufacturing technology.

The electronics plant was, for instance, designed with 280 different workstations requiring the use of 5,000 different machines and/or tools. There were 30,000 different parts and about 1,000 sub-groups of components. This meant dealing with 2,000 suppliers. This vertical integration, with its complex technological dissimilarity, is illustrated in Tables 4.1, 4.2, 4.3 and 4.4. The farm machinery plant was also designed to produce thirty three different end-products. The engines and tractors plant, with 3,446 employees and seven large workshops using a wide range of technologies, was designed to produce ten different end-products.

This has led to a high degree of technology dissimilarity amongst these plants. This is on top of extremely subservient behaviour towards the Central Plan, a poorly qualified workforce and low support in terms of national policy for promoting technological development and innovation. Even more difficult to cope with is the 'manufacturing of components', rather than the manufacture of end products, as it demands a rather different set of scientific, engineering and production principles. Manufacturing components does not facilitate the understanding and the assimilation of these different technical specialisations either. As a consequence of this vertical integration and its complexity, necessary knowledge of basic information such as waste control, operation management, overall lead time, rate of rejects and re-work, is often lacking.

This high degree of technology dissimilarity also means that a large proportion of raw materials has to be imported from abroad. The lack of management expertise and the long bureaucratic procedures for imports often result in a chronic shortage of raw materials and uncertainty in deliveries. This is why NEEI and NEFM are forced to maintain large inventories (6–11 months). The overall effect is of an enduring and strong external dependency in terms of raw materials, components and machinery.

Both organisations seem to have developed their own technological solution based on developing a complete manufacturing system through three complementary phases. The first phase consists of importing, installing and operating manufacturing systems. This can be viewed as a radical innovation because of the major technological changes it brings to the user organisation. The second phase is the rationalisation and optimisation of the first phase installations. This is small and incremental innovation.

The third phase, in reality, is a combination of radical and incremental innovation. Its objective is to prepare the organisations to deal effectively with new and advanced technology based on information technology. The major changes this brings could be considered as radical innovation inasmuch as it requires new processes and equipment. However, both companies have attempted to integrate the new and advanced technology into the systems, technology and capability already in existence. In doing this they have assumed any additional risk of incompatibility would be avoided and have ignored affects on learning and performance. This then explains why the third phase is viewed as both incremental and radical innovation.

The success of such an approach is notably linked to the existence of a certain level of local capability. As Bell (1982, 1984) points out, the rate of assimilation of imported technical systems depends on the nature and magnitude of the domestic stock of manpower having the capacity and ability to manipulate the technology involved in these systems.

The scarcity of local competence and skill has meant a lack of local managers able to participate in activities such as the choice, implementation and even the initial operation of imported technology. This is emphasised by authors such as Tlemcani (1983) and Perrin (1983) when they state that Algerian firms are 'passive consumers of imported technology'. Imported technology has in fact been regarded as a consumable item rather than a set of machines and processes that are evolving and dynamic. In the two firms studied, the substantial level of technological capacity necessary for the effective assimilation of imported technology was not available. This lack of qualified and trained workers must be one of the major reasons for the incompatibility between the imported technology, perceived as complex by the users, and the poorly skilled context in which it is operated. This low level of in-house skill is also related to the persistent lack of organisational adaptations to new requirements, such as a flatter type of organisational structure, a better and quicker flow of communication and the decentralisation of decision-making to places where information is located.

Simply buying the physical aspect of technology is not enough and can even be inappropriate and counter-productive. Indeed, research in developed countries has highlighted that the main reason underlying failure to secure the full potential benefits of advanced technology is the lack of organisational adaptation. A substantial level of benefits is often achieved not from acquisition of equipment but rather by changing organisational practice through simplification and rationalisation activities. Schonberger (1982) and Jones (1990) claim that the superiority of Japanese manufacturing is often derived from their superior organisation. The messages emerging from such findings therefore seem clear and can be summarised as follows.

i.   The use of advanced technology is incompatible with traditional organisational arrangements such as those adopted by companies from developing countries such as NEEI and NEFM.

ii.   Simple and low cost organisational alterations based on flexibility, decentralisation communication and interaction can enable organisations from developing countries to avoid repeating the mistakes of the past with respect to transfer of technology and ensure that they get the best out of the new systems of technology.

3. Mismatch between Technology and Environment

The market places in most developing countries are characterised by large changes in product range and a higher frequency of change occur. In this context, in spite of the protection against competition guaranteed by the state, NEEI has been unable to sell its products because of their obsolescence. The general expectation is that, electronic consumer goods will be put on the market in a wide range and replaced within a very short time. However, it took NEEI more than 10 years to replace obsolete goods such as radios, cassette players, and record players because of their mono-function design. While the tendency is now towards more miniaturisation and integration of multiple functions leading to the replacement of many components by a single one, the mechanical design of NEEI's products is based on the use of heavy and large dimension printed circuits such as the Medium Scale Integration (MSI) replaced on the international market by Large Scale Integration (LSI). The silicon plates of two and three chips still manufactured in NEEI are also out of date and elsewhere have been replaced by more integrated, reliable and economical silicon plates of five and six chips.

As described in Chapter 4 , these examples of obsolescence are the result of a choice made in the 1970s where Fordist principles and mass production guided management approaches. In this manufacturing process, the intensification of work was supposed to be the result of the workers' subordination to machines. Shopfloor workers were only engaged in operation activities such as direct handling or processing of products. The mass production option required high investment in plants and machinery tools designed to carry out specific operations and was therefore associated with a particular product. The choice of such a system is based on low variety production and is motivated by the need to improve productivity through high volumes of output.

As business has now shifted towards continuous improvement and innovation to deal with increasing changes, both NEEI and NEFM have been attempting to build up a greater ability to deal with variety and flexibility by the acquisition of advanced technology machine tools. This is why the plant for tractors and engines has installed a flexible cell to manufacture two types of engine-blocks and two types of gear boxes to replace three old machine tools. A CNC machine has also been acquired to take charge of activities such as grinding and boring carried out previously by two different machine tools. An automated assembly line has replaced semi-automated and manual activities in the assembly and control of end-product. In the farm machinery, a flexible cell, NC and CNC machines have also been purchased to replace several old machine tools.

Similarly, in order to overcome the obsolescence identified in its manufacturing system and to improve the reliability of its products, NEEI in its 'Redeployment' programme has heavily invested in computer-aided processes for design and manufacturing of major electronic components such as semi-conductors, condensers and cathode ray tubes and in CNC for press and moulding activities. They have also purchased advanced IT applications for assembly and control of end-products with the belief that it would increase quality and reliability, reduce production times and increase volume of production.

It can be argued that within both state-owned companies there is an awareness of the need to respond quickly and frequently to market changes. However, the ability to adapt to new requirements is considered attainable only through the acquisition of the appropriate technological hardware. The organisation of production, based on Taylorist mass-production principles, remains unchanged in both firms, i.e. task fragmentation and standardisation with specialist departments responsible for planning and designing every operator's tasks. Their major objective is still increasing the productivity through an increase of volumes and efficient capacity utilisation. Both firms are still clearly committed to an approach based on the notion that the high costs associated with the acquisition of expensive machine tools can be recovered using mass production techniques. Improving production capacity seems to be the major goal of the acquisition and implementation of advanced technology as it was during the 1970s with the transfer of conventional technology.

In practice, the installation of new machine tools and their integration with the old system of technology has led to considerable bottlenecks obstructing the use of production capacity, extending the production lead time and reducing the rate of productivity. This results from an incompatibility between skills required for the operation of new technology and the current model of organisation designed for mass production purposes. That model is based on 'one man one task' for as long as the market is considered as predictable and certain. However, the new technology offers the possibility to carry out various functions via an integration of tasks. This integration requires the introduction of multi-skilling and team-work. The emphasis on flexibility leads also to the necessity of variable skill which means continuous training and retraining. The key determinants for success of, i.e. adequate skills and appropriate organisational arrangements are still lacking in most companies from developing countries such as Algeria.

The analysis of the implementation of new models of organisation (Chanaron and Perrin, 1987; Posthuma, 1990) suggests that the use of advanced technology has led to a radical change in the labour process. This change is the result of the shift from a model of organisation strongly based on separation of the conception and the execution of work, and the subordination of workers to machines, to a situation where workers are required to prepare, monitor, and maintain the machine. The role of workers in the old model of organisation is limited to handling and processing products whereas a successful implementation of an advanced technology system requires a strong participation of shopfloor workers in gathering and analysing data and making decisions concerning the manufacturing activities. The effective use of this new type of technology requires from workers an understanding of the whole system and a participative role in problem-solving at the production line. Operators are, for instance, required to take responsibility for identifying errors and correcting them and also identifying causes of failure and breakdowns and even proposing solutions to avoid mistakes. The incompatibility identified in NEEI and NEFM is thus the consequence of the use of advanced technology by workers with low knowledge and competence in an organisational context still influenced by Fordist principles. Transfer of advanced technology is unlikely to succeed unless the organisational context is altered.

4. The Nature of the New Solution

This section outlines the changes required by the new forms of organisation in order to reduce incompatibility and to secure the best of the imported technology. Piore and Sabel (1984) report that new manufacturing priorities based on non-price factors as described by De Meyer *et al.*(1987), need a new organisational approach, that mass production organisation, characterised by division of labour and rigid bureaucracy is unable, to offer. Rush(1989) and Bessant (1990) argue that the new solution needs a closer working relationship between the different departments of a business and the dismantling of boundaries. Jacobson *et al.* (1983) considers the new approach in terms of systems, taking into consideration all the interactions between technology, labour and organisational arrangements. The removal of boundaries and the need for co-operation and communication imply adaptations of skills, structures, procedures, and even culture (Lui *et al.*, 1990; Cartwright, 1999).

4.1. Division of Work

The use of advanced technology has led to a change from a situation where workers are subordinated to machines and concerned with simple and repetitive operation activities, to a situation where the workers' main task is to monitor and maintain the machine. The new machine is now in charge of basic operational activities. This radical change of the process of labour in the new organisation of work has very often enabled firms to reap most if not all of the potential benefits of the new technology (Schonberger, 1982; Simmonds and Senker, 1990). However, in the two companies in the case study, advanced technology is running in the context of mass production organisation. New technology machine tools were purchased to renew the old manufacturing facilities and to increase output and reliability. These new machines were combined with a conventional system of production operating under Fordist practices and procedures. Although the new technology tools provide workers with the opportunity to take charge of regulation activities, little initiative and responsibility is given to shopfloor workers. The system is therefore still based on separation of the conception and execution functions. The control and co-ordination are completed through formal mechanisms, structures, and procedures. This separation between 'head and hand' constitutes one of the major obstacles, to the efficient use of new technology in developing countries. Indeed with specialisation and division of work, decision-making is not located where information is available and this often slows the production process and militates against commitment and involvement of the workforce (Nutt, 1986; Posthuma,1990). Without involvement and commitment, new technology is unlikely to be accepted and successfully implemented (Leonard-Barton, 1988).

4.2. Regulation and Co-ordination

The use of advanced technology has led to a shift from monitoring and co-ordinating simple and repetitive activities to a situation where shopfloor supervisors and plant managers have to monitor and co-ordinate regulation activities. This requires a shift in the structure of employment towards more qualified and skilled workers. The impossibility of fulfilling such a requirement in the short term is used by managers from NEEI and NEFM to justify the current use of the Fordist model of organisation. The absence of responsibility and initiative at the level of shopfloor workers is explained by the low level of in-house competence and experience. This corresponds, to some extent, to the situation at the beginning of the 20th century with the emergence of mass production and its emphasis on the separation of functions and fragmentation of tasks to simplify work and make it accessible to the unskilled workforce employed in US factories.

4.3. Adaptation to Changes

The capacity to adapt to environmental changes – ignored by Taylor for whom the environment was completely predictable – is now becoming a vital element for firms' survival. This new need has led to the development of a new production system combining efficiency and flexibility and hence affecting the whole business. Organisational changes are concerned essentially with responses to shifts in work organisation, such as those brought about by removing the separation of execution and conception functions and the consequent impact on hierarchical levels and procedural control. The need for a firm to be efficient and flexible leads to a structural shift based on functional integration, with close relationships between different departments. The removal of boundaries between departments and similar activities leads to the emergence of team-work and to a need for co-ordination between the different groups. Unlike the traditional model, this co-ordination is performed via informal mechanisms and procedures. With the set up of team-work, there is also a need for new structural arrangements with fewer levels of hierarchy and a better flow of communication.

The accomplishment of such organisational changes requires first the ability to choose and operate technology efficiently, and second the ability to manage changes in manufacturing processes, procedural and organisational arrangements. This corresponds to the definition of assimilation proposed by Bell (1984) which includes (a) a progressive development of domestic supply of technological and managerial inputs for future investment projects; and (b) a progressive expansion of decision making and managerial control over the process of incorporating technology into investment projects.

An efficient transfer of technology is undoubtedly linked to the assimilation of the imported technology. Approaches conducive to assimilation must include investment in technological capability, especially in the human and institutional capital needed to initiate, absorb and manage technological change. This would lead to enhancing the level of skill and competence of firms and enable them to undertake changes corresponding to their level of assimilation, that is incremental changes which forms the essence of understanding and effective development of capabilities in developing countries.

5. The Relevance of the New Solution to Firms from Developing Countries

The approach adopted by NEEI and NEFM has led to a manufacturing situation typical of a large number of firms from developing countries and is characterised by the following factors:

i.   breakdowns delay;
ii. poor and inadequate maintenance;
iii. waiting for parts, tools or fixtures;
iv. time wasting in adjusting tools;
v.   queuing problems at bottleneck operations;
vi. low machine utilisation downstream of bottlenecks;
vii. high rate of scrap and low quality;

viii. high inventory levels of raw materials and work in process;
ix. unreliable deliveries of raw materials;
x. long production lead time;
xi. low productivity;
xii. shortage of in-house skill;
xiii. too many layers of supervision and unsuitable organisational structure;
xiv. poor worker involvement;
xv. absence of autonomy leading to excessive paper work and to a lack of management commitment;
xvi. absence of good and long term relationships with suppliers.

Most of these problems are described as typical of firms neglecting organisational adaptations and can be addressed by a systematic approach based on rationalisation and simplification of work.

In this context and in order to implement a simple solution, Katz (1984) suggests that firms from developing countries should seek the reduction of the production time. They should pursue simplification of production design, reduction of handling time and more adequate management. Jacobson and Sigurdson (1983) argue for good internal and external communication, a top management commitment to search for best practice and an acceptance of risks. They also indicate the importance of having a long-term corporate strategy and corporate flexibility and responsiveness to change.

Given the problems facing organisations from developing countries, and the solutions suggested, it appears that the approach to adopt is associated with optimisation and rationalisation of existing potentialities. Firms from developing countries should, for instance, have no reason to retain so many hierarchical layers without efficient co-ordination and communication. Why do they agree to pay for supplies which are not going to be used for another 6 to 12 months? Why do they also keep ignoring the heavy cost of inventory? Why are they continually in conflict with their foreign suppliers – especially when 90% of their raw materials come from abroad?

There is also a vital need to develop a new set of norms and practices to support a new cultural and organisational approach conducive to effective participation, sharing of information, joint-learning and co-operation as the prevailing culture in most firms from developing countries is perceived as inhibiting innovation and the full exploitation of advanced technology.

Chapter 9
Technology Transfer: a dynamic process of learning and organisational adaptation

Technology transfer is a highly complex phenomenon involving many different functions, actors and variables forming a process which is not reducible to simple factors. Its success is rarely associated with doing one or two things outstandingly, but rather with performing all functions effectively and in a balanced and integrated manner. The study of innovation theory has highlighted the importance of implementation, which is viewed as a dynamic process of mutual adaptation between the technology and its environment. This interaction is extended to the scientific, social, economic, institutional and cultural spheres. This renders any attempt to provide a prescription for successful innovation, and hence a specific mode of development for industrialising countries, a particularly complex task.

The examination of the use of new technology systems in developed countries has indicated difficulties surrounding its implementation, many of which are related to the organisational context. The problem is further complicated in developing countries where technology is often viewed as an item or a piece of hardware bought and transported from one place to another, regardless of the cultural, social, economic and organisational context of the host company and country.

Introduction of new and advanced technology in developing countries is unlikely to succeed unless the approach and the organisational context are modified. This approach must take into account the restricted availability of technical knowledge and information and the vast number of social, organisational and economic features which can make it difficult or impossible to replicate off-the-shelf, organisational design or technology previously developed and used in industrialised countries. This suggests a strong emphasis on the need for a different selection environment and different technology trajectories for firms in developing countries which may lead to a combination of traditional and new models of organisation and the search for cultural elements to include in any organisational re-arrangements in order to ensure a greater compatibility between the imported technology and its micro and macro environment and better commitment of the workforce at all levels. This requires a gradual shift from the current mechanistic and bureaucratic approach to a flexible and organic type of organisation which will allow a more participative role in problem-solving, greater responsibility and initiative and a better flow of communication and exchange of information. Greater autonomy and responsibility should, therefore, be offered to firms as well as to individuals in order to take into consideration all relevant specifics and to release their potential, creativeness and initiatives.

The limited level of scientific, engineering and managerial background in developing countries is bound to affect the pool of knowledge and information to be gained from the process of technology transfer. There are three major types of information needed for an effective implementation and operation of imported technology. The first is viewed as the key to learning about an innovation and is related to process know-how, engineering expertise and product design capabilities. This core information is very closely protected by suppliers in order to maintain their market lead. The second type of information is that which is always transferred, e.g.: as operating procedures. The third type is rarely willingly transferred but at least "open to negotiation". Collaboration with technology suppliers and lasting relationships built on mutual benefits can guarantee the transfer of the third type of information.

The lack of scientific and engineering background can only be solved in the long-term by substantial and continuous investments in education, research and training and the generation of adequate local national systems for the promotion of innovation. In the short and medium term, and in the context of increasing globalisation, joint-venture and greater collaboration with technology suppliers can ensure access to information, understanding and expertise.

The impact of the lack of this scientific and engineering background may also be attenuated by exploring the possibility of horizontal technology transfer between users as indicated in Figure 9.1. This horizontal collaboration and sharing of information and expertise can be facilitated and championed by the state, local and regional authorities and associations. It can also be envisaged within institutions such as the Organisation of African Countries, North African Countries, West African Countries, and Latin American Countries in order to promote technology transfer between developing countries.

The debate is no longer about whether or not to adapt organisations to technology but when to adapt , that is simultaneously, prior to or after implementation, in order to secure the maximum potential benefits from the use of new technology. A new technology system should not be introduced purely for productivity improvements, but for a wider set of objectives affecting the performance of the entire organisation.

Technology transfer like innovation is not a single action, but rather a total process involving all the activities of bringing a new idea to the market and characterised by notable interfaces. It is a highly complex phenomenon where changes are of techno-economic and social type since they affect not only engineering activities but also various facets of management and organisation activities. It brings a new way of thinking and calls for changes throughout the entire business. Here again, success depends on several simultaneous factors. At the level of firms, the introduction of such innovation calls for a new 'techno-economic paradigm' or a new 'post-Fordism wave' built on principles such as flexibility, co-operation,

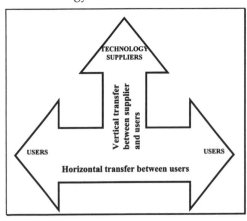

Figure 9.1: Horizontal transfer between users of technology

co-ordination, participation, commitment, better flow of communication, flatter organisational structures, team work, integration and removal of boundaries between functions and activities. However, there is no single best solution and the approach adopted by a firm will not be static but rather adaptable to new requirements and need not be similar to those adopted by other firms operating in the same country or industry.

It is therefore vital for companies from developing countries to seek a market niche in an environment where business strategies are increasingly orientated towards globalisation where market needs and requirements are changing constantly and rapidly, and where the industry is characterised by a high proliferation of advanced technology. The definition of this market niche strategy could be associated with the acquisition of a more appropriate and less complex technology. The use of advanced technology should not be neglected but should be conceived with a good and lasting collaboration with technology suppliers.

An effective transfer of new technology depends on the completion of the five major steps outlined below.

a.   The selection of technologies – demands that potential users have an awareness of each individual element of the technology to be imported. Jacobson and Sigurdson (1983) point out that these potential users should have sufficient knowledge and understanding of the specific application of the new technology in their own sectors. They would therefore benefit from, and indeed need, an up-to-date flow of relevant information in order to opt for what Rosenberg (1982) describes as an 'intelligent choice'. Such choice procedures enable a good fit between the technology and the organisation to be achieved.

b.   Mechanisms for technology transfer – These concern: (a) the acquisition, (b) the establishment of a licence agreement with respect to process know-how, product know-how, managerial expertise and technical services, and (c) the purchase of equipment.

c.   Operating technology at the designed capacity – Once the technology has been appropriately selected and transferred, the question arises as to how to utilise it to ensure performance at the designed level. An early involvement in doing 'things', i.e. learning-by-doing, is necessary but it must be combined with other forms of acquiring knowledge and skills, such as training, searching and the hiring of foreign expertise. The inclusion of these forms of learning has proved to be of major importance in the use of those new technology systems characterised by continuous change.

There is also a need here to consider macro-economic factors, such as an appropriate education and curriculum (including the establishment of links between universities and higher schools and industry) subcontracting, and maintenance networks.

d.   Adapting technology to local conditions – After installation and assimilation, it is often necessary to adapt imported technology to local requirements and specifications. These adaptations must include the operation of machinery as well as managerial procedures and will require skill and understanding. The effective use of the learning forms discussed above and collaboration with foreign experts ensures this important step is successful.

e.   Generating technology – An objective for Developing Countries must be to move towards the new generation of technology and to be able to cope with the changes this will bring. The newly industrialised countries of South Korea, Brazil and India have shown this can be done successfully when appropriate attention is given to steps (a),(b), (c) and (d) described above.

The successful completion of each of these steps requires a wide range of skills for activities such as feasibility studies, project management, preliminary choice of production, acquisition and construction of process and product technologies, engineering, construction, commissioning and initial operation, including maintenance and detailed engineering and design. A certain level of in-house knowledge and competence is a necessary condition for the effective assimilation of any imported technology. This requirement is even higher when importing advanced technology and, even more specifically, information technology. Here workers are dealing with regulating and maintaining machines rather than merely accomplishing simple and repetitive tasks; responsibility and initiative may be given to shop-floor workers who gather and analyse information and make decisions. Technology transfer is a dynamic process and its successful implementation in developing countries requires continuous learning and organisational adaptations.

Bibliography

Argyris, C. (1964) *Integrating the Individual and the Organisation*, John Wiley , New York.

Argyris, C. and Schon, D. (1980) 'What Is an Organisation that It May Learn' in Lockett, M. and Spear, R. (eds), *Organisation as Systems*, Open University Press, Milton Keynes.

Arnold, E. (1894) 'CAD in Europe', Science Policy Research Unit/ Sussex European Research Centre Report No. 6, Sussex University.

Barrow, A. (1989) 'The Acquisition of Technological Capabilities in the Korean CNC Machine Tool Industry', PhD thesis, University of Edinburgh.

Bell, M. (1982) 'International Transfer of Industrial Technology and Incremental Technical Change in Industrialising Countries', Second Conference on Technology and Industrial Policy in China and Europe, University of Sussex, 27–30 September.

Bell, M. (1984) 'Learning and the Accumulation of Industrial Technological Capacity in Developing Countries' in Fransman, M. and King,K (ed.), *Technological Capability in the Third World*, Macmillan, London.

Bell, M., Ross-Larson, B. and Westphal, L.E. (1984) 'Assessing the Performance of Infant Industries', World Bank Staff Working Papers No. 666,Washington.

Benachenhou, A. (1980) *Planification et Développement en Algerie: 1962–1980*, SNED, CREA, Algeria.

Benachenhou, A. (1982) *Developpement et Coopération internationale*, Office des Publications Universitaires, Algeria.

Benissad, M.E. (1982) *Economie du développement de l'Algerie: Sous Developpement et Socialisme*, Economica, 2nd edn, Algeria.

Berkowitz, L. (1954) 'Group Standards, Cohesiveness, and Productivity', *Human Relations*, November, pp. 509–19.

Berlo, D.K. (1960) *The Process of Communications.*, Holt, Rinehart and Winston, New York, pp.30–2.

Bessant, J. (1982) 'Influential Factors in Manufacturing Innovation', *Research Policy*, 11, pp. 117–32.

Bessant, J. (1986) 'UK Experience with Computer-Aided design – an overview', Report prepared for the Manufacturing Industries Branch of the ILO, Innovation Research Group, Business School, Brighton Polytechnic.

Bessant, J. (1990) *Fifth Wave Manufacturing: Management Implications of Advanced Manufacturing Technology*, Blackwell, Oxford.

Bessant, J. and Buckingham, J. (1991) 'Organisational Learning for Effective Computer-Aided Production Management', Centre for Business Research, Brighton Business School, Brighton Polytechnic, January.

Bessant, J. and Grunt, M. (1985) *Management and Manufacturing Innovation in the UK and West Germany*, Gower Press, Aldershot.

Bessant, J. and Lamming, R. (1990) *Dictionary of Production Management and Technology*, Macmillan, London.

Betz, Z. F. (1987) *Competing through New Ventures, Innovation, And Corporate Research*, Prentice-Hall, Englewood Cliffs, NJ.

Bigoness, W. J. and Perreault, W. D.(1981) 'A Conceptual Paradigm and Approach for the Study of Innovators', *Academy of Management Journal*, 24 (1).

Bolton, M., K. (1993) 'When Is Necessity the Mother of Invention?: Organisational Innovation in Successful and Unsuccessful Firms'in Cozzijnsen and Vrakking (eds), *Handbook of Innovation Management*, Blackwell Business.

Boutaleb, G. (1980) 'Approfondir la Coherence de la Planification', *Revolution Africaine*, 13 September, Algeria.

Bouyacoub, A. (1987) *A la Gestion de l'Entreprise Industrielle Publique en Algerie*, Vol. 1, Office des Publications Universitaires, Algeria..

Bouzidi, A.(1986) 'L'evolution du Statut de l'Entreprise Publique Algerienne dans la Politique Nationale de Developpement Economique', *Actes du Symposium*, 6/8 December, Algeria.

Burns, B. (1988) 'Integrating Technology, Integrating People', *Production Engineer*, September, pp. 54–6.

Burns, T. and Stalker, G. (1966) *The Management of Information*, Tavistock, London.

Camgni, R.,(1991) 'Introduction: from the Local "Milieu" to Innovation through Co-operation Networks' in Camgni, R.(ed.), *Innovation Networks: Spatial Perspectives*, Belhaven Press, London.

Carter, C.F. and Williams, B.R. (1957) *Industrial and Technical Progress*, Oxford University Press, Oxford.

Cartwright, J., *Cultural Transformation – Nine Factors for Improving the Soul of Your Business*, Financial Times, Prentice-Hall, 1999

Cawson, (1996) 'Networks and Inter-Firm Collaboration' in Dodgson,, M. and Rothwell (eds), *The Handbook of Industrial Innovation*, Edward Elgar, Cheltenham.

Chen, M., (1996) *Managing International Technology Transfer*, Thomson Business Press.

Child, J. (1977) *Organisations*, Harper and Row, London.

Clark, N. and Juma, C. (1987) *Long-Run Economics: an Evolutionary Approach to Economic Growth*, London/New York, Pinter Publishers.

Coombs, S R., Saviotti, P. and Walsh, V. (1987) *Economic and Technological Change*, Macmillan Education.

Cooke, P., and Morgan, K.(1993) The Network Paradigm: New Departures in Corporate and Regional Development' in *Regional Science*, Vol. 74, 4, pp. 317–40.

Cooper, C. (1980) 'Policy Intervention for Technology Innovation in Developing countries' in World Bank Staff Working paper No.441, Washington, DC, December.

Cooper, C. and Hoffman, K. (1981) 'Transactions in Technology and Implications for Developing Countries', Science Policy Research Unit and Institute of Development Studies, University of Sussex.

Cooper, C. and Maxwell, P. (1975) 'Machinery Suppliers and the Transfer of Technology to Latin America', Report by the Science Policy Research Unit to the Organisation of American States, Washington, DC.

Coulson-Thomas, C., (1997) *The Future of the Organisation – Achieving Excellence through Business Transformation*, Kogan Page, London.

Dahlman, C.J and Fonseca, F.V.1978 'From Technological Dependence to Technological Development: the Case of the Usiminas Steel Plant in Brazil', IDB/ECLA/UNDP/IDRC Regional Program of Studies in Scientific and Technical Development in Latin America, Working Paper 12, Buenos Aires.

Dahlman, C. J. and Westphal, L. (1982) Technological Effort in Industrial Development: a Survey in Stewart, F. and James J, *The Economics of New Technology in Developing Countries*, France Printer Publishers.

Bibliography

Dahlman, C. J., Ross-Larson, B. and Westphal, L.E. (1987) 'Managing Technological Development, Lessons from the Newly Industrialising Countries',World Bank Staff Working Papers No.717, Washington.

Dahmani, A.M. (1985) *L'Engineering dans la maîtrise industrielle et Technologique*. Office des Publications Universitaires, Algeria.

De Meyer, A., Nakane, J., Miller, J.G. and Ferdowski, K. (1987) 'Flexibility: the Next Competitive Battle Manufacturing', Roundtable Research Report Series. Boston, University School of Management, February.

Dempsey, P. (1982) 'New Corporate Perspectives in FMS' in Rathmill, K. (ed.), *Proceedings of FMS-2 Conference*, Kempston, IFS Publications.

Department of Employment, *Employment for the 1990s*, Cm 540, HMSO, December.

Destanne de Bernis, G. (1966) 'Industries Industrialisantes et Contenu d'une Politique d'Intégration Régionale, in *Economie Appliquée*, Nos 3–4.

Destanne de Bernis, G. (1968) 'Role du Secteur Public dans l'Industrialisation', *Revue Economique*.

Destanne de Bernis, G. (1970) 'Quelques Observations au sujet des Biens d'Equipements dans un Processus General d'Industrialisation et de Développement National fondé sur la Transformation des Hydrocarbures', *Colloque Des Economistes Arabes*, Algeria.

Dodgson, M.,(1996) 'Technological Collaboration' in Dodgson, M. and Rothwell R (eds), *The Handbook of Industrial Innovation*, Edward Elgar, Cheltenham.

Dosi, G. (1982) 'Technological Paradigms and Technological Trajectories', *Research Policy*, Vol. 11, No.3, pp.147–62.

Dosi, G. (1984) *Technological Change and Industrial Transformation: the Theory and Application to the Semiconductor Industry*, Macmillan, London.

Dosi, G. (1988) 'The Nature of the Innovation Process', in Dosi *et al.* (eds) op.cit.

Dosi, G. and Orsenigo, L.(1988) 'Market Structure and Technical Change' in Heertj A. (ed.), *Innovation, Technology and Finance*, Oxford, Basil Blackwell.

Dosi, G., Teece, D., and Winter, S.(1987) 'Towards a Theory of Corporate Coherence', paper presented at the Conference on Technology and Firms in a Historical Perspective, Terni, Italy, 14 October.

Dosi, G., Freeman, C., Nelson, R., Silverberg, G. and Soete, L. (eds) (1988) *Technical Change and Economic Theory*, Frances Pinter, London.

Ebrihampour, M. and Shonberger, R. (1984) 'Japanese Just in Time/Total Quality Control System of Production: Potential for developing Countries', *International Journal of Production Research*, 22, pp.421–30.

Economic Bulletin for Europe, 'Flexible Manufacturing: a Step Towards Computerized Industrial Automation', *The Journal of the United Nations Economic Commission for Europe*, Vol. 37, No. 3, September.

Enos, J. (1958) 'Measure of the Rate of technological Progress in the Petroleum Refining Industry', *Journal of Industrial Economics*, 6, pp. 180–97.

Ferraz, J.C. (1984) 'Technical Development and Conditioning Factors: the Case of the Brazilian Shipbuilding Industry',PhD thesis, Sussex University.

Fiedler, F.E. (1967) *A Theory of Leadership Effectiveness*. New York, McGraw-Hill.

Fleck, J.(1983) 'Robotics in Manufacturing Organisations' in Winch (ed.) op.cit.

Foyer, P.(1985) 'Profitable Manufacturing Systems' in Lindholm R.(ed.), Proceedings of the 4th International Conference on FMS, Sweden, 15-17 October.

Fransman, M.(1986) *Technology and Economic Development, Sources of Technical Change*, Wheatsheaf, Brighton.

Fransman, M. and King, K.(1984) *Technological Capability in the Third World*, Macmillan Press, London.

Freeman, C. (1967) 'Chemical Process Plant: Innovations and the World Market', *National Institute Economic Review*.

Freeman, C. (1974) *The Economics of Industrial Innovation*, New York. Penguin Books.

Freeman, C. (1987) *Technology Policy and Economic Performance: Lessons From Japan*, London, Frances Pinter.

Freeman, C. (1996) 'Innovation and Growth' in Dodgson M. and Rothwell R (eds), *The Handbook of Industrial Innovation*, Edward Elgar, Cheltenham.

Freeman, C. and Perez, C. (1988) 'Structural Crises of Adjustment, Business Cycles and Investment Behaviour' in Dosi G. *et al.* (eds), *Technical Change and Economic Theory*, Frances Printer, London.

Freeman, C., Clark, J. and Soete, L.(1982) *Unemployment and Technical Innovation: a Study of Long Waves and Economic Development*, Frances Pinter, London.

Galbraith, J. (1973) *Designing Complex Organisations*, Addison-Wesley, Reading, MA.

Georghiou, L., Metcalfe, J.S, Gibbons, M., Ray, Y T. and Evans, J. (1986) *Post Innovation Performance: Technological Development and Competition*,.Macmillan, London.

Gibbons, M. and Johnson, R. (1974) 'The Role of Science in Technological Innovation', *Research Policy*, 3, pp. 220–42.

Girvan, N., P. and Marcell, G. (1990) 'Overcoming Technological Dependency: te Case of Electric (Arc) (Jamaica) Ltd., A Small Firm in s Small Developing Country', *World Development*, 18, pp. 91–107.

Glover, J.W.D and Rushbrooke, W.G (1983) *Organisation Studies*, Nelson BEC Books.

Gold, B., Rosegger and Boylan (1980) *Evaluating Technological Innovations*, Lexington Books, Heath D. C. & Co, Lexington, Mass. and Toronto.

Goumeziane, S. (1994) *Le Mal Algérien: Economie Politique d'une Transition Inachevée*, Fayard,

Granstrand, 0., Hakannson, L. and Sjolander, S. (1992) *Technology Management and International Business*, John Wiley, Chichester.

Grindley, P. (1993) 'Firm-Strategy and Successful Technological Change' in Cozijnsen and Vrakking (eds), *Handbook of Innovation Management*, Blackwell Business, London.

Gruenfeld, L.W and Foltman, F.F.(1967) 'Relationships among Supervisors' Integration, Satisfaction, and Acceptance of a Technological Change' *Applied Psychology*, 51.

Guzzo, R.A.(1986) 'Group Decision Making and Group Effectiveness in Organisations' in P.S Goodman and Associates, *Designing Effective Work Groups*, Jossey-Bass, San Francisco, pp. 34–71.

Hassan (1996) *Algérie Les Raisons d'un Naufrage*, Seuil.

Hellweg, S.A. and Phillips, S.L (1980) 'Communication and Productivity in Organisations: a State of-the-Art Review' in Proceedings of the 40th Annual Academy of Management Conference, Detroit, Michigan, pp.188–92.

Herzberg, F., Mausner, B. and Snyderman, B.B. (1959) *The Motivation to Work*, John Wiley, Chichester.

Bibliography

Hobbay, M. (1996) 'Innovation in Semiconductor Technology: the Limits of the Silicon Valley Network Model' in Dodgson, M. and Rothwell, R.(eds), *The Handbook of Industrial Innovation*, Edward Elgar, Cheltenham.

Hoffman, K. and Girvan, N. (1990) 'Managing International Technology Transfer. a Strategic Approach for Developing Countries', IDRC, April.

Hveem, H(1978) 'Technology and Contradiction between Internationalisation of Capital and National Development: Some Notes on the Case of Algeria', International Peace Research Institute Publications, No. S 21/78, pp.213–20.

The Institution of Production Engineers (1980) *Current and Future Trends of Manufacturing Management and technology in the UK – the Way Ahead*, The Institution of Production Engineers, Rochester House, London.

The Institution of Production Engineers, *Innovation in Manufacture*, London.

Jacobsson, S. and Sigurdson, J. (eds) (1983) *Technological Trends and Challenges in Electronics*, Lund University.

Jaikumar, R. and Bohn, E.R. 'The Development of Intelligent Systems for Industrial Use: a Conceptual Framework', *Research on Technological Innovation, Management and Policy*, 3, pp. 169–211.

Jewel, L.N. and Reitz, H.J.(1891) *Group Effectiveness in Organisations*, Scott, Foresman, Glenview, IL.

Johnson, B. and Rice, R. (1987) *Managing Organisational Innovation: the Evolution from Word Processing to Office Information Systems.*,Columbia University Press, New York.

Jones, D.T.(1990) 'Beyond the Toyota Production System: the Era of Lean Production', Paper presented at the 5th International Operations Management Association Conference on Manufacturing Strategy, Warwick, 26–27 June.

Juma, C. (1986) 'Evolutionary Technological Change: the Case of Fuel Ethanol in Developing Countries', DPhil thesis.

Kahn, R. and Katz, Z D. (1960) 'Leadership Practices in Relation to Productivity and Morale' in Cartwright D. and Zander A. (eds), *Group Dynamics: Research and Theory*, 2nd edn, Row, Paterson.

Kanter, R. (1996) *World Class: Thriving Locally in the Global Economy*, Simon and Schuster, New York.

Kaplinsky, R.(1980) *Computer-Aided-Design*, Frances Pinter, London.

Kaplinsky, R. (1984) *Automation*, Longman, London.

Kast, F.E. and Rosenzweig, J.E. (1985) *Organisation and Management: a System and Contingency Approach*, 4th edn, McGraw-Hill.

Katz, J. 'Domestic Technology Generation in Less Developed Countries: a Review of Research Findings', IDB/ECLA Research Programme in Science and Technology.

Katz, J. (1981) 'Technology Innovation, Industrial Organisation and Comparative Advantages of Latin American Metalworking Industries' in Fransman, M. and King, K., *Technological Capability in the Third World Countries*, Macmillan Press, London.

Katz, J. (ed) (1982) *Technology Generation in Latin American Manufacturing Industries*, Macmillan, London.

Katz, J. (1984) 'Domestic Technological Innovations and Dynamic Comparative Advantages: Further Reflections on a Comparative Case Study Program', *Journal of Development Economics*, Vol .16, Nos 1/2, September-October.

Kendrick, J.W. (1984) *Improving Company Productivity; Handbook with Case Studies*, The John Hopkins University Press, Baltimore.

Knight, K.D. (1963) 'A Study of Technological Innovation: The Evolution of Digital Computers', DPhil Thesis, Carnegie, Institute of technology, Pittsburgh.

Kuhn, T. (1962) *The Structure of Scientific Revolutions*. University of Chicago Press, Chicago.

Kuznets, S. (1965) *Economic Growth and Structure: Selected Essays.*,W.W. Norton, New York.

Lall, S. (1982) *Developing Countries as Exporters of Technology: a First Look at the Indian Experience*, Macmillan Press, London.

Lall, S., (1992) 'Technological Capabilities and Industrialisation', *World Development*, Vol. 20, No.2.

Lall, S. *et al.* (1994) *Technology and Enterperise Development: Ghana under Structural Adjustment*, New York: St. Martin's Press.

Lambright, W.H. (1980) *Technology Transfer to Cities*, Westview Press, Boulder, Co.

Lamming, R. and Bessant, J.(1987) *Dictionary of Business and Management*, Macmillan, London.

Landes, D. (19869) 'A Characteristic Approach to Technological Evolution and Competition. Manchester' University of Manchester, mimeo.

Langrish, J., Gibbons, M., Evans, W., and Jones, F. (1972) *Wealth from Knowledge*, London Macmillan.

Lawrence, P. and Lorsh, J. (1967) *Organisation and Environment.*,Harvard University Press, Boston, MA.

Leonard-Barton, D. (1988) 'Implementation and Mutual Adaptation of Technology and Organisation',. *Research Policy*, 17 (5), pp. 251–77.

Leonard-Barton, D. (1990) 'Modes of Technology Transfer within Organisations: Point-to-point Versus Definition', *Production and Operations Management*, Harvard Business School, Boston MA, May.

Leonard-Barton, D. (1991) 'The Factors as Learning Laboratory', Harvard Business School Working Paper, No. 92-023, Boston, MA.

Leonard-Barton, D. and Deschamps, I.(1988) 'Managerial Influence in the Inplementation of New Technology', *Management Science*, Vol. 34, No. 10, October.

Liu, M., Denis, H., Kolodny, H. and Stymne, B. (1990) 'Organisation Design Technological Change', *Human Relations*, Vol. 43, No. 1, pp. 7–22.

Lundvall, B. (1990) *National Systems of Innovation: Towards a Theory of Innovation and Interactive Learning*, Frances Pinter, London.

Marceau, J. (1996) 'Another Determinant – Clusters, Chains and Complexes: Three Approaches to Innovation with a Public Policy Perspective' in Dodgson, M. and Rothwell, R (eds), *The Handbook of Industrial Innovation*, Edward Elgar, Cheltenham.

Mansfield, E.(1968) *The Economics of Technical Change*, Norton, New York.

Martin, R. *et al* . (1985) 'Some Human Factors in Effective CAD', *CAE Journal*, February.

Mascerenhas, R.C.(1982) *Technology Transfer and Development: India's Hindustan Machine Tools Company*, Westview Press, Boulder, CO.

Mayo, E. (1933) *The Human Problems of an Industrial Civilization*, Macmillan, New York, 1933.

McGrath, J.C. (1933) *Groups: Interaction and Performance*, Prentice-Hall, Englewood Cliffs, NJ.

Mensch, G. (1979) *Stalemate in Technology: Innovations Overcome the Depression*, Ballinger Publishing Co., Cambridge, Mass.

Morgan, K. (1997) 'The Learning Region; Institutions, Innovation and Regional', *Regional Studies*, No. 31.5, pp.491–503.

Bibliography

Mowery, D. and Rosemberg, N. (1979) 'The Influence of Market Demand upon Innovation: a Critical Review of Some Recent Empirical Studies', *Research Policy*, 8.

Myers, S. and Marquis, D.G. (1969) 'Successful Industrial Innovation', National Science Foundation, Washington, DC.

Nabseth, L. and Ray, G.(1974) *The Diffusion of New Industrial Processes*, Cambridge, Cambridge University Press.

National Science Foundation(1983) 'The Process of Technological Innovation Reviewing the Literature', May .

Nellis, J.R. (1980) 'Maladministration, Cause or Result of Underdevelopment?: the Algerian Example', *Revue Canadienne des études Africaines*, March.

Nelson, R. (ed.) (1993) *National Innovation Systems*, Oxford University Press, Oxford.

Nelson, R. and Winter, S. (1977) ' In Search of Useful Theory of Innovation' in *Research Policy*, 6, pp. 36–76.

Nelson, R. and Winter, S. (1978) 'Innovation and Economic Development: Theoretical; retrospect and Prospect', IDB/CEPAL Studies on Technology and Development in Latin America.

Nelson, R. and Winter, S.(1982) *An Evolutionary Theory of Economic Change*, Harvard University Press, Cambridge, MA.

New, C. and Myers, A. (1986) *Managing Manufacturing Operations in the UK 1975–1985*, British Institute of Management/Cranfield Institute of Technology, Bedford.

Nicholas, I., Warner, W., Sorge, A. and Hartmann, G. (1983) 'Computerized Machine Tools, Manpower Training and Skill Polarisation: a Study of British and W.German Manufacturing Firms', in Winch,G. (ed.) op.cit.

Nutt, P. (1986) 'Tactics of Implementation', *Academy of Mangement Journal*, 29 (2), pp. 230–61.

Osterkamp, R. (1982) 'L'Algerie entre le Plan et le Marché: Points de vue recents sur la Politique Economique de l'Algerie', *Canadian Journal of African Studies*, Vol. 16 (1) 2, pp. 27–42..

Parker, J.E.S. (1974) *The Economics of Innovation: the National and the Multinational Enterprise in Technological Change*, London, Longman.

Pavitt, K. (1984a) 'Technology, Innovation and Strategic Management', Brighton Science Policy Research Unit, University of Sussex, mimeo.

Pavitt, K. (1984b) 'Patterns of Technological Accumulation', *Research Policy*.

Pavitt, K.(1985) 'Patent Statistics as Indicators of innovative Activities and Problems', *Scientometrics*.

Pavitt, K. (1987) 'On the Nature of Technology', Inaugural Lecture, Science Policy Research Unit, Sussex University, 23 June.

Pavitt, K, Robson, M. and Townsend, J. (1987) 'The Size Distribution of Innovating Firm in the UK:1945–1983', *Journal of Industrial Economics*.

Peck and Otto, *Government Co-ordination of R&D in the Japanese Electronics Industry*, Yale University, New Haven, Conn.

Pelz, D.C. and Munson, D. 'The Innovations Process: a Conceptual Framework', Ann Arbor, MI: Working Paper, Center for Research on Utilisation of Scientific Knowledge, University of Michigan.

Perez, C. 1984) 'Microelectronics, Long Waves and World Structural Change', *World Development*, Vol. 13, No. 3, pp. 441–63.

Perrin, J. (1983) *Les Transferts de Technologie*, La Decouverte/ENAL, Paris.

Perrow, C.(1967) 'Framework for the Comparative Analysis of Organisations', *American Sociological Review*, Vol. 32.

Pior, M. and Sabel, C. (1984) *The Second Industrial Divide*, Basic Books, New York.

Porter, M. (1990) *The Competitive Advantage of Nations*, Macmillan Press, London.

Porter, M. (1996) 'Competitive Advantage, Agglomeration Economies, and regional Policy, in *International Regional Science Review* 19, 1 & 2 pp 85-94, 1996.

Posthuma, A. (1990) 'Japanese Production Techniques in Brazilian Automobile Components Firms: A Best Practice Model or Basis for Adaptation?', paper presented at the Conference on Organisation and Control of the Labour Process, Aston University, 28–30 March.

Ray, G.F. and Uhlmann, L.(1979) 'The Innovation Process in the Energy Industries', National Institute of Economic and Social Research, Occasional Paper No. 30, Cambridge University Press, Cambridge.

Rhodes, E. and Wield, D. (1985) *Implementing New Technologies – Choice, Decision and Change in Manufacturing*, Blackwell, Oxford, and Cambridge, MA.

Rice, R.E. and Rogers, E.M. (1980) 'Re-Invention in the Innovation Process', *Knowledge*, 1, pp. 499–514.

Rickards, T. (1985) *Stimulating Innovation: a System Approach*, London, Frances Pinter.

Rodriges, C. A.(1985) 'A Process for Innovators in Developing Countries to Implement New Technology', *Colombia Journal of World Business Research*, pp.21–26.

Rogers, E. (1983) *The Diffusion of Innovations*, 3rd ed.n, New York, Free Press/Macmillan.

Rogers, E. and Schoemaker, F. (1971) *The Communication of Innovations*, Free Press, New York.

Rogers, E., Eveland, J.D. and Klepper, C.A. (1977) 'The Innovation Process in Public Organisation: Some Elements of a Preliminary Model', Final Report to National Science Foundation (Grant RDA 75-177952).

Rosegger, G. (1980) 'The Economics of Production and Innovation: an Industrial Perspective', Pergamon Press, London.

Rosenberg, N. (1976) *Perspectives on Technology*, Cambridge University Press, Cambridge.

Rosenberg, N. (1979) *Learning by Using*, Stanford University, Stanford.

Rosenberg, N. (1982) *Inside the Black Box: Technology and Economics*, Cambridge University Press, New York.

Rothwell, R. (1977) 'The Characteristics of Successful Innovators and Technically Progressive Firms', *R&D Management*, 7 (3), pp 191–206.

Rothwell, R. (1986) 'Innovation and Re-Innovation: a Role for the User', *Journal of Marketing Management*, No. 2, pp. 109–23.

Rothwell, R. (1988) 'The Successful Innovative Firm: Some research results', paper presented at the European Conference on Regional Development, Innovation and Technology. Bilbao, Spain, 27–28 October.

Rothwell, R. (1992) 'Successful industrial innovation: critical success factors for the 1990s, *R&D Management*, 22 930, 221–39

Rothwell, R., Teubal, M., Pablo, T. and Townsed, J. (1976) 'Methodological Aspects of Innovation Research – Lessons from a Comparison of Project SAPPHO and FIP', Science Policy Research Unit, Sussex University, 1976.

Rousseau, D. M. and Cooke, R. A. (1984) 'Technology and Structure: the Concrete, Abstract, and Activity Systems of Organisations', *Journal of Management*, 10 (3), 1, pp. 345–61..

Bibliography

Rush, H. (1989) *Diffusion of Advanced Manufacturing Manufacturing Techniques: an Overview, Centre for Business Research*, Brighton Business School, Brighton Polytechnic.

Ruttan, V. (1959) 'Usher and Schumpeter on Invention, Innovation and Technological Change', *Quarterly Journal of Economics*, November, pp. 596–606.

Saad , M. (1991) 'The Transfer and the management of New technology: The case of two Firms in Algeria', PhD Thesis, University of Brighton.

Said, Amer T. (1978) *L'Industrialisation en Algerie*, Anthropos.

SAPPHO (1974) 'Success and Failure in Industrial Innovation', Report on SAPPHO project by Science and Policy Research Unit of Sussex University.

Sassi, Y. and Chenouf, S. (1986) 'Une Reflexion sur la Gestion Des Resources Humaines Dans le Cadre de La Restructuration des Entreprises', *Actes Du Seminaire National Sur La Restructuration des Entreprises Publiques*, Union Des Sociologues et Des Economistes Algeriens, Oran, January..

Schon, D.A. (1967) *Technology and Change: the New Heraclitus*, Delacorte Press, New York.

Schonberger, R.(1982) *Japanese Manufacturing Techniques*, Free Press/Macmillan, London.

Schmookler, J. (1972) 'Technical Change and the Law of Industrial Growth' in Griliches, Z. and Hurwicz, L. (eds).

Schumpeter, J.A. (1934) *The Theory of Economic Development*, Harvard University Press, Cambridge, Mass.

Schumpeter, J.A. (1938) *Business Cycles: a Theoretical, Historical and Statistical Analysis of the Capitalism Process*, Vol. 1, McGraw-Hill, New York

Schumpeter, J.A. (1942) Capitalism Socialism and Democratie, Harper, New York.

Senge, P. (1991) *The Fifth Discipline*, Doubleday, New York,1991.

Senker, P. and Arnold, (1982) 'Designing the Future: the Skills Implications of Interactive CAD', Occasional Paper No. 9, Engineering Industries Training Board, Watford.

Shaw, (1996) 'User/Supplier and Innovation', in Dodgson, M. and Rothwell, R. (eds), *The Handbook of Industrial Innovation*, Edward Elgar, Cheltenham.

Simmonds, P. and Senker, P.(1989) 'Computer-Aided Engineering in the 1980s: a Report on a Longitudinal study in British Engineering Companies', Report prepared for The Engineering Industry Board. Science Policy Research Unit, Sussex University, February.

Simpson, L. (1959) 'Vertical and Horizontal Communication in Formal Organisations', *Administrative Science Quarterly*, pp .188–9.

Solo, R.A. and Rogers, E. M.(eds) (1972) *Inducing Technological Change for Economic Growth and Development.*,Michigan State University Press, East Lansing, MI.

Solow, R. (1957) 'Technical Change and the Aggregate Production Function', *Review of Economics and Statistics*, Vol.39.

Stewart, F. (1981) 'Indigenous Technical Change in Third World Countries' in Fransman, M. and King, K. (eds), *Technological Capability in Third World*, Macmillan Press, London.

Stewart, F. and James, J. (1982) *The Economics of New Technology in Developing Countries*, France Printer, London.

Stewart, C. and Nihei, Y. (1987) *Technology Transfer and Human Factors*, Lexington Books, Lexington, Mass.

Strassman, W.P. (1959) *Risk and Technological Innovation: American Manufacturing Methods during the 19th Century*, Cornell University Press.

137

Swords-Isherwood, N. (1984) 'The Process of Innovation: a Study of Companies in Canada, the United States and the United Kingdom', The British–North American Committee, London.

Teubal, M. (1984) 'The Role of Technological Learning in the Exports of Manufactured Goods–the Case of Selected Capital Goods in Brazil', in *The Role of Technological Learning*, pp.105–130.

Teubal, M., Arnon, N. and Trachtenberg, M.(1976) *The Falk Innovation Project (FIP)*.

Tidd, J., Bessant, J. and Pavitt, K.(1997) *Managing Innovation: Integrating Technological Market and Organisational Change*, John Wiley, Chichester.

Tlemcani, R.(1986) *State and Revolution in Algeria*, Westview, Boulder, CO, London.

Trist, E. (1981) 'The Evolution of Socio-Technical Systems: a Conceptual Framework and an Action Research Programme', Occasional Paper No. 2, QWL, Ontario.

Tuckman, B.W. (1965) 'Developmental Sequence in Small Groups', *Psychological Bulletin*, May, pp. 384–399.

UNIDO (1975) *Guidelines for the Acquisition of Foreign Technology, with Special Reference to Licensing Agreements*, UNIDO Technology Division.

Usher, A. (1954) *History of Mechanical Invention*, Harvard University Press, Cambridge, Mass.

Utterback, J.M. *et al.* (1973) *The Process of Innovation in Five Industries in Europe and Japan*, .: Centre for Policy Alternative, Cambridge, Mass..

Von Hippel, E. (1976) 'The Dominant Role of Users in the Scientific Instrumentation Innovation Process', *Research Policy*, Vol. 5, No. 3, pp. 212–39.

Von Hippel, E.(1988) *The Sources of Innovation*, Oxford University Press, New York.

Voss, C.A. (1985) 'The Need for a Theory of Implementation of Innovation', ESRC Conference, Cumberland House, May.

Voss, C.A. (1986) 'Implementing Manufacturing Technology: a Manufacturing Strategy Perspective' in Voss, C.A. (ed.), *Managing Advanced Manufacturing Technology*, IFS Publications, Kempston.

Voss, C.A.(1991) 'The Process of Implementation of New Processes', *Business Strategy Review*.

Voss, C.A. (1992) 'Successful Innovation and Implementation of New Processes', *Business Strategy Review*, Vol. 3, No. 1, Spring, pp. 29–44.

Vrackking, W. (1993) 'Strategic Innovation Moments' in Cozijnsen and Vrakking (eds), *Handbook of Innovation Management*, Blackwell Business.

Waitsos, C. V. (1974) *Intercountry Income Distribution and Transnational Enterprises*, Clarendon Press, Oxford.

Walsh, V., Roy, R., Potter, S. and Bruce, M.(1992) *Winning by Design: Technology, Design and International Competitiveness Product*, Basil Blackwell, Oxford.

Westney, D. E. (1994) 'The International Transfer of Organisational Technology' in Edward K.Y. Chen (ed), *Technology Transfer to Developing Countries*, UNCTAD, New York.

Winch, G., and Voss, C., A. (1991) 'The Process of Implementation: the Evaluation Stage', Operations Management Working Paper, London Business School, London.

Woodward, J. (1965) *Industrial Organisation*, Oxford University Press, Oxford.

Yachir, F. (1983) *Technologie et Industrialisation en Afrique*, Office des Publications Universitaires, Algeria.

Zaltman, G., Duncan, R.B. and Holbek, J. (1973) *Innovations and Organisations*. New York, John Wiley.

Zeleny, M., (1989) High Technology Management, *Human Systems Management*, 6, 109-120.